LEGACIES

OF

THE TEN FOUND TRIBES OF ISRAEL

Donald Miller

DIFFERENT PERSPECTIVES PUBLISHING INC.™

Published by

Different Perspectives Publishing Inc.
Wyomissing, PA 19610

www.differentperspectivespublishing.com

You are wholeheartedly invited to please enjoy the reading.

Publisher's Cataloging-in-Publication
(Provided by Quality Books, Inc.)

Miller, Donald, 1936 Apr. 6-
    Legacies of the ten found tribes of Israel / Donald Miller.
    p. cm.
    Includes bibliographical references and index.
    ISBN-13: 978-0-9797050-0-7
    ISBN-10: 0-9797050-0-2
    1. Lost tribes of Israel.   I. Title.
DS131.M55 2007   909'.04924
                         QBI07-600174

Cover designed by Jan Abramowicz
Reading Eagle Press

Printed and bound in the United States of America
by Reading Eagle Press

PREFACE

At a time when the armed forces of the United States began fighting the Talaban in Afghanistan a television news report of the fighting included an interview with an elder of the Pashtoon People. These people were settled all over Afghanistan but were concentrated mostly around the southeastern city of Kandahar. This elderly gentleman was telling the reporter that he and his people, the Pashtoon People, were descendants of the Ten Lost Tribes of Israel. He said it proudly and gave some evidence in the form of his customs that appeared to have been Hebraic. He seemed to have been a very credible kind of individual and I believed him and suspect that the news media believed him too, or else he probably wouldn't have been on nationwide television.

Intrigued by the possibility that descendants of the Ten Lost Hebrew Tribes were in evidence in the modern day world, I began a study of the Ten Lost Tribes of Israel: who they were and where they came from; and that led to an understanding of the chronology of the tribes from the time of the Patriarchs to the Return to Zion and the disappearance of the tribes as such.

I was fortunate to have the book, A HISTORICAL ATLAS OF THE JEWISH PEOPLE edited by Eli Barnavi, Reference 2, on my reference shelf and used it as my chief source of information for the history found in Section I as well as the visual aids shown in the Section I figures.

The second part of the study involved the search for the people of the Ten Lost Tribes and that was accomplished by looking at three anomalies found in the chronology; and then by looking into those anomalies a picture of what the world of the Ten Lost Tribes of Israel could have looked like emerged.

The first anomaly related to the Judeans who had been exiled to Babylonia during the Babylonian exile occurring in 597 and 586 B.C.E., and that anomaly centered around how so many of those Judeans prospered in Babylonia in such a short period of time, between the first exile and the Return to Zion in 538 B.C.E., a period of about 59 years, with no visible means of support.

The second anomaly related to King Cyrus of Persia who in 530 B.C.E. having gone to Chorasmia beyond the most northern part of the Persian Empire, died there fighting the Scythians. The question underlying this anomaly is: 'Why would this powerful king go to this supposed no man's land to fight and get killed'?

The third anomaly related to King Cyrus' later successor, King Darius I, who finally conquered Chorasmia along with the two other northern territories of Armenia and Thrace as well as acquiring, in previous Persian conquests, the northern and eastern parts of Egypt and North Africa along the Mediterranean Sea and south along the Red Sea all the way to the Jewish city of Yeb. It seems reasonable for the Persians to want to conquer those parts of Egypt and North Africa for purposes of trade, but why would they be interested in the 'unknown' lands of the north.

Looking at the third anomaly, the conquest of the northern territories of Thrace, Armenia and Chorasmia through modern maps of that region and then searching those maps for anything that appeared to be Hebraic the Alay Mountain Range was found. A modern Hebrew to English dictionary, Reference 1, showed that the word alay means 'above me, around me'; and so this first entry into the study found a Hebrew word, alay, meaning 'above me, around me' gave a Hebraic meaning to the Alay Mountain Range of Central Asia.

Pinpointing several other cities having Hebraic sounding names and applying that same technique did not result in as meaningful results as its application to the Alay Mountains. The Aramaic, Arabic, Greek, Latin, Russian, Polish, English, German, and whatever other languages that had gotten into modern Hebrew had to be filtered out in order to get to the Biblical Hebrew language spoken by the Samarians, the people of the Ten Lost Tribes.

Being fortunate in finding the Jastrow Dictionary, A DICTIONARY OF THE TARGUMIM, THE TALMUD BABLI AND YERUSHALMI, AND THE MIDRASHIC LITERATURE by Professor Marcus Jastrow, Reference 4 in the bibliography, provided the turning point in the study. Besides giving the English definitions of Hebrew words occurring in the Jewish Bible and Talmuds, Professor Jastrow identified the sources of the words along with other important notations, and he cross referenced words having similar meanings but different spellings or different consonantal sequences.

With this Biblical and post Biblical Hebrew to English dictionary necessary for continuation of the study in hand, those Hebraic sounding names on the modern maps not well defined in the modern Hebrew to English dictionary were reexamined using the Jastrow Dictionary and this time pay dirt was hit.

Using the Jastrow Dictionary, a word analysis process developed. This analysis included finding Hebraic sounding names on the maps, transliterating them into Hebrew letters and then breaking down those transliterations into groups of consonants having consonantal sequences similar to those found in the Jastrow Dictionary. Those words were identified as Hebrew root words and their definitions found in the Dictionary were added up in logical sequences and meaningful English definitions of those transliterated into Hebrew names emerged as English equivalent names of the ancient Samarian settlements. This process is better described technically in Section II as the Hebrew 'word analysis'.

The proofs incorporated into this study were brought about by using the Hebrew 'word analysis' to establish the distributions of the meanings of names of the cities and places on the modern maps that show the itineries of those abducted Samarians and the world of their descendants, the names given to other peoples and places by them and/or their descendants, the names that their Barbarian Descendants gave to themselves and others, the names given to the eastern religions and their doctrines which have Hebrew 'word analysis' definitions similar to modern English descriptions of those names and doctrines and Hebrew 'word analysis' definitions of English names and words and names and words in and of other languages correlating, in unexpected ways, with English descriptions and translations coming from other independent sources. This is a mouthful that will become clearer as one proceeds through the rest of this writing.

The 'maps' shown in FIGURES I-1 through I-5 and FIGURE II-5 should be considered as visual aids rather than cartographic devices. Although the bodies of water and rivers are fairly specifically placed with respect to each other in those visual aides, and should be used as reference points, the cities and places are merely generally placed and should be considered as descriptors backing up the text.

In FIGURE II-5 the cities shown in blue are those determined to have been the original settlements of abducted Samarians, and those shown in orange are determined to have been named after the settlements had developed, taking on names of what those settlements were noted for.

The italicized text shows the author's comments and suppositions while the text in regular font shows points of fact that are referenced either to outside sources or to proofs shown in this writing.

The term B.C.E. (Before the Common Era) is a secular form of the term B.C.; and the term C.E. (Common Era) is a secular form of the term A.D.

Although all of the text was prepared using a word processor, all of the visual aids and Hebrew 'word analyses' were prepared in a computer graphics application. This process required a considerable amount of 'eye balling'. The disparages in the font and line forming and spacing within the graphics are the result of the author's moving of text from the word processor into the graphics application, 'eye balling' the development of the graphics' compositions and then moving the graphics back into the word processor. 'Next time' I should know better.

Donald Miller

TABLE OF CONTENTS

SECTION I – CHRONOLOGY OF THE TRIBES FROM THE PATRIARCHS TO THE RETURN TO ZION AND THEIR FINAL DISAPPEARANCE

1800 to 1700 B.C.E. – This was the time of Abraham, Isaac and Jacob and Jacob's twelve sons; when Jacob's oldest sons sold their younger bother Joseph into slavery in Egypt where Joseph rose to prominence in the court of the pharaoh. A 'family reconciliation' resulted in the movement of all of Jacob's family to Egypt. In Egypt, each of the brothers: Reuben, Simon, Levi, Judah, Issachar, Zebulun, Dan, Naphtali, Gad, Asher and Benjamin founded a tribe having their respective names. Joseph, however, did not found a tribe but his two sons, Ephraim and Manasseh did. By the time of the Exodus these thirteen tribes, the descendants of Jacob, whose other name was Israel, had grown into a nation, the Nation of Israel, including large numbers of people.

1300 to 1200 B.C.E. – During this time Moses lead the thirteen tribes, The Children of Israel, in the Exodus out of Egypt and into the Sinai Desert; and Joshua, Moses' successor as the leader of the People of Israel, settled the tribes into the land of Canaan often using terror tactics to displace the Canaanites.

1100 to 1000 B.C.E. – The tribes were settled as twelve tribes in twelve geographical regions in The Land of Israel with each of the tribes having a territory of its own except for the Levites, the priestly tribe, which settled in Levitical cities scattered among the twelve geographical tribes. The names of the twelve tribes are shown in blue in FIGURE I-1. The red boundary shown in that figure is the boundary of the State of Israel as determined by the Israeli 1948 War of Independence and can be used to visualize the territorial extent of the original Land of Israel, the land of the thirteen tribes.

1029 to 1007 B.C.E. – The twelve geographical tribes united under a king, Saul of the tribe of Benjamin, who secured the borders of the new Kingdom of Israel; but according to Biblical records King Saul and his sons died in battle with the Philistines in attempting to reclaim Hebrew tribal lands from them.

1000 B.C.E. – According to those same Biblical records, David of the tribe of Judah was elected King of Israel. He defeated the Philistines and expanded the territories of the Kingdom. The gold boundary line in FIGURE I-2 shows the expanded boundary accredited to and ruled by Kings David and Solomon.

967 B.C.E. – King David died and was succeeded by his son Solomon who established a period of heavy building which included many fortified cities and Solomon's First Temple in Jerusalem.

928 B.C.E. – King Solomon died and his son Rehoboam succeeded him. With the death of King Solomon the northern tribes of Asher, Naphtali, Issachar, Zebulun, Manasseh, Gad, Simon, Reuben, Dan and Ephraim under Jeroboam, Son of Nebat of the tribe of Ephraim seceded from the Kingdom of Israel and founded the Northern Kingdom, also named Ephraim, Israel and Samaria, leaving the Kingdom of Judah in the south.

A long war between the Kingdoms of Judah and Samaria lasting until the latter part of that century allowed previously subjugated territories to regain their independence and left the two kingdoms considerably reduced in size with respect to the Kingdom of David and Solomon, FIGURE I-3.

During the Ninth Century B.C.E. both kingdoms reached a compromise and divided the contended boundary consisting of the territories of the tribes of Benjamin and Dan with most of Dan going to Samaria and most of Benjamin going to Judah; and then both kingdoms regained much of the territories that they had previously lost, with Edom in the south being reclaimed by the Kingdom of Judah; and Aram, Ammon and Moab in the north and east being reclaimed by the Kingdom of Samaria, FIGURE I-3.

Then both kingdoms collaborated in the building of a fleet of ships in Ezion Geber at the head of the Red Sea, a city that is believed to be near the modern Israeli city of Elath.

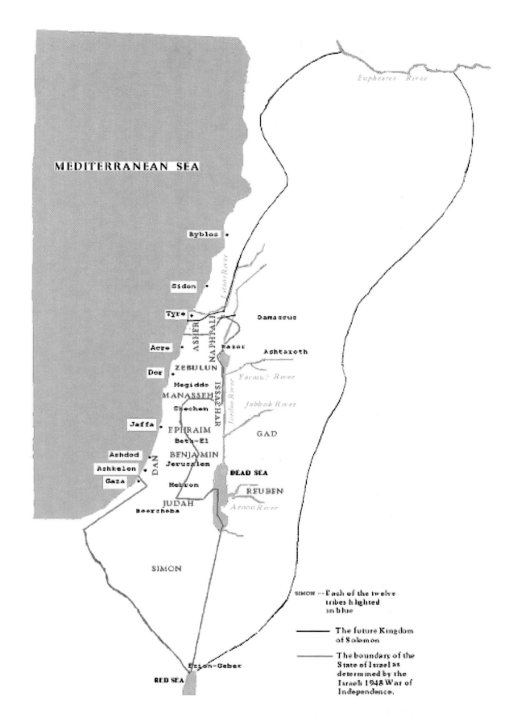

TERRITORIES OF THE SETTLED TRIBES IN THE 12TH - 11TH CENTURIES B.C.E. COMPARED TO MODERN ISRAEL

FIGURE I - 1

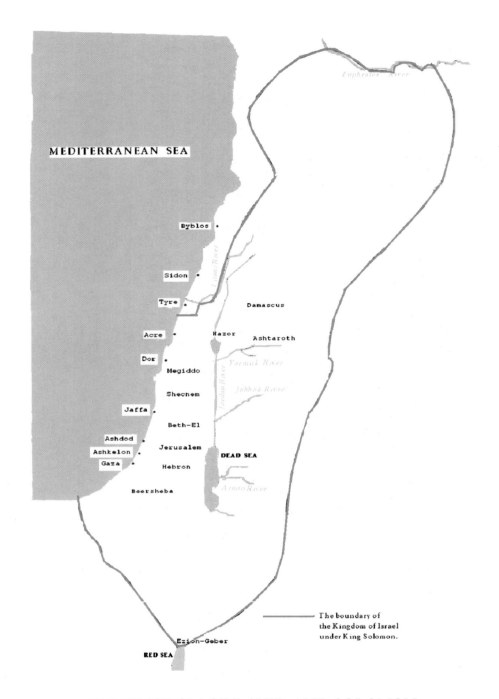

MEDITERRANEAN SEA

Byblos •

Sidon •

Tyre •

Damascus

Acre •   Hazor

Ashtaroth

Dor •

Megiddo

Shecnem

Jaffa •

Beth-El

Ashdod •

Ashkelon •   Jerusalem

Gaza •   Hebron

DEAD SEA

Beersheba

—— The boundary of
the Kingdom of Israel
under King Solomon.

Ezion-Geber

RED SEA

THE KINGDOM OF DAVID AND SOLOMON

FIGURE I - 2

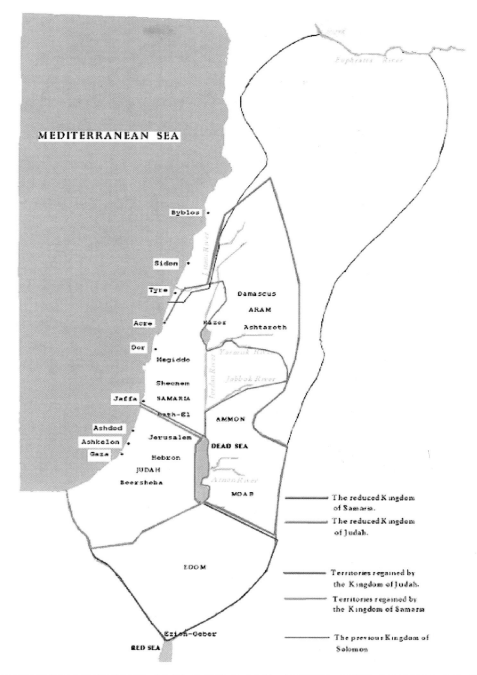

THE VARIOUS KINGDOMS OF ISRAEL AFTER THE DEATH OF KING
SOLOMON

FIGURE I - 3

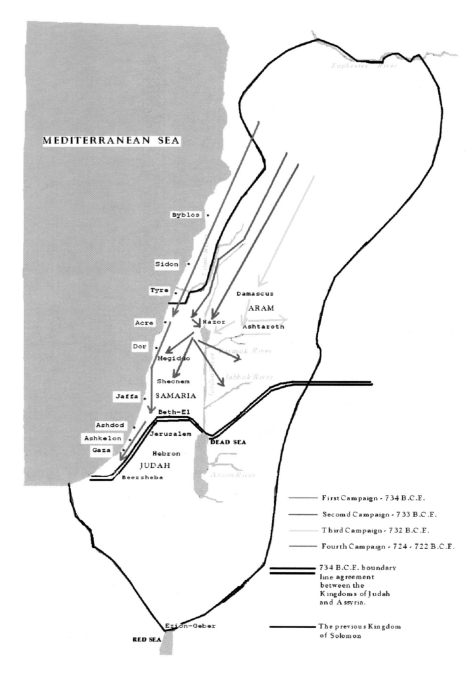

MEDITERRANEAN SEA

Byblos

Sidon

Tyre

Damascus

ARAM

Acre   Hazor

Ashtaroth

Dor

Megiddo

Shechem

Jaffa   SAMARIA

Beth-El

Ashdod

Ashkelon   Jerusalem   DEAD SEA

Gaza

Hebron

JUDAH

Beersheba

——— First Campaign - 734 B.C.E.

——— Second Campaign - 733 B.C.E.

——— Third Campaign - 732 B.C.E.

——— Fourth Campaign - 724 - 722 B.C.E.

══ 734 B.C.E. boundary
line agreement
between the
Kingdoms of Judah
and Assyria.

——— The previous Kingdom
of Solomon

Ezion-Geber

RED SEA

THE CAMPAIGNS OF ABDUCTION AFTER THE FALL OF THE KINGDOM OF SAMARIA TO ASSYRIA

FIGURE I - 4

6

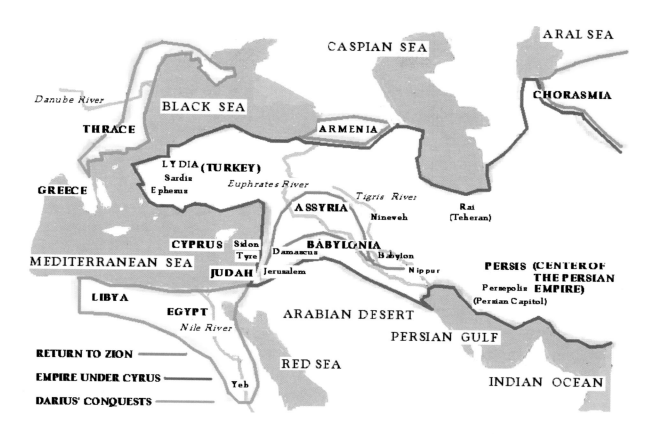

THE PERSIAN EMPIRE IN THE 6TH - 5TH CENTURIES B.C.E.

FIGURE I - 5

737 B.C.E. – The Kingdom of Samaria with its neighboring Kingdom of Arom had been vassal states of the Assyrian Empire since 738 B.C.E. and urged the Kingdom of Judah to join them in an alliance against Assyria. Judah did not join those kingdoms and in 734 B.C.E. Assyria fully defeated the two kingdoms, reached an agreement with the Kingdom of Judah over their boundary and began its campaign of control over Samaria and Arom.

734 to 722 B.C.E. – In four campaigns beginning in 734 B.C.E. and ending in 722 B.C.E., FIGURE I-4, Assyria took the most skilled people into captivity and left the least skilled; and 'back filled' the abducted people with Aramaic speaking peoples from other lands taken by the Assyrians; and their language,

7

Aramaic, replaced the Hebrew that was spoken by the Samarian People. The abducted Samarians are known as the 'Ten Lost Tribes of Israel'.

598 to 597 B.C.E. – The Babylonians, who had now conquered the Assyrians, overran Jerusalem, the capital of the Kingdom of Judah, and carried off into exile in Babylonia people from leading families as well as 'skilled' persons leaving a 'puppet' king at the throne of Judah.

586 B.C.E. – Jerusalem was again overrun by the Babylonians because of actions taken by the 'puppet' king, and the city as well as Solomon's Temple were destroyed and a further part of the remaining population was taken into exile in Babylonia leaving only those with 'little skills'. This turmoil sent many Judeans fleeing to Egypt and there establish the city of Yeb. In Babylonia, both waves of exiled Judeans prospered, and kept their religion but they as the Judeans left behind in Judah began speaking Aramaic as did those who had fled to Egypt. The only people still using Biblical Hebrew in their everyday vernacular could have been the abducted Samarians, if they were allowed to remain unassimilated into larger cultures.

539 B.C.E. – The conquest of Babylonia by Persia resulted in a less harsh policy by Cyrus, the King of Persia; and in 538 B.C.E. the Cyrus Proclamation was issued which allowed for the return of Judeans to Jerusalem. The Return to Zion was begun with the funding of several thousands of the less prosperous exiled Judeans in Babylonia by more prosperous ones to rebuild the city of Jerusalem and Solomon's Temple, Solomon's Second Temple. As seen in FIGURE I-5 the Return to Zion, shown with red lines, followed two routes. The more northern route followed the Tigris River to the route's northern most point and then came down overland past Damascus to Jerusalem. The more southerly route followed the Euphrates River to that route's northern most point and then went south overland past Damascus to Jerusalem almost as though both routes followed already existent trade routes with which the Judeans were familiar.

530 B.C.E. – King Cyrus of Persia was killed fighting the Scythians in Chorasmia, FIGURE I-5.

486 B.C.E. – By this time King Darius I of Persia, a successor to King Cyrus, had conquered a good part of Egypt extending west through Libya and south to and somewhat beyond the Jewish city of Yeb as well as the three northern territories of Thrace, Armenia and Chorasmia shown outlined in orange lines in FIGURE I-5.

SECTION II – THE SEARCH FOR THE PEOPLE OF THE LOST TRIBES USING TRANSLITERATED DEFINITIONS

The search centered on the northern lands acquired by King Darius I of Persia, which are at this writing the Central Asian and European republics newly freed from the now former Soviet Union. Using modern maps of those geographical areas many cities and regions having Hebraic sounding names were found.

To determine the English definitions of those Hebrew sounding cities and regions, the following word analysis, graphically shown in FIGURE II-1 and herein called the Hebrew 'word analysis', was performed.

1. The accepted English spelling for the name or word being analyzed was acquired and a brief description of it was added.

2. That name or word was transliterated from English into Hebrew.

3. The Hebrew root words of the transliteration were eked out and those Hebrew root words, found most usually in the Jastrow Dictionary, were words with consonantal sequences similar to those extracted from the Hebrew transliteration. These Hebrew root words were placed onto a worksheet similar to that shown in FIGURE II-1 along with excerpts of the English definitions found in the, most usually, Jastrow Dictionary that had the potential to fit into meaningful definitions of the cities', places' or peoples' names. In addition to root word definitions containing parentheses placed by Professor Jastrow, the author also used square brackets, [.....], in root word definitions to bring literal definitions into more modern terminology.

4. Those root words were added together and their consonants compared to the consonants in the transliterated Hebrew names or words. Consonants were used and vowels ignored because according to Webster's Unabridged Dictionary, Reference 12, in the English Language the language changes with each generation but the major changes are in the vowels with consonants remaining constant. Expecting that all languages including Hebrew undergo

10

those same language transformations, then it was surmised that ancient Hebrew, both Biblical Hebrew and 'Aramaic Hebrew' should retain their consonants in the modern languages derived from them. These modern languages have different sounds and words than the original Hebrew but the roots of the words and their consonantal sequences remain the same.

5. 'Loose' consonants found in Step 4 are shown in red and were 'analyzed' as the transliterated into Hebrew words were 'analyzed' in Step 3. Those 'loose' lettered words took on the 'NOT!' meaning in the final definitions of the names and words and are also shown in red.

6. The final definitions were a logical array of the most meaningful definitions found in Steps 3 and 5, meaningful with respect to what one would have expected those words, in ordering the array of definitions, to have the most logical meanings. The words in parentheses were put in for the convenience of modern colloquialism.

The following abbreviations are used throughout the study:

b.h. = Biblical Hebrew – The Hebrew language as written and spoken by Hebrews in Biblical times before and during the abductions of the 'Ten Lost Tribes' by the Assyrians.

p.b.h. = post Biblical Hebrew – Language including Aramaic, spoken by Hebrew People in the Kingdom of Judah and in Babylonia after the exile of Judeans from the Kingdom of Judah by the Babylonians to Babylonia beginning in 597 B.C.E. and not placed into the Torah when it was redacted in or around 495 B.C.E. This also includes words foreign to Biblical Hebrew placed into the vernacular more recently.

Jastrow = English definitions of Hebrew words found in the Jastrow Dictionary.

Webster = English definitions of Hebrew words found in Webster's Hebrew Dictionary.

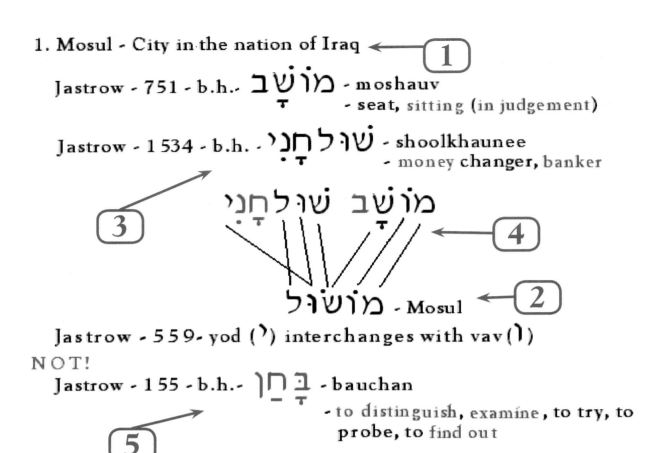

1. Mosul - City in the nation of Iraq ← ①

Jastrow - 751 - b.h. - מוֹשָׁב - moshauv
 - seat, sitting (in judgement)

Jastrow - 1534 - b.h. - שׁוּלְחָנִי - shoolkhaunee
 - money changer, banker

③ → מוֹשָׁב שׁוּלְחָנִי ← ④

מוֹשׁוּל - Mosul ← ②

Jastrow - 559 - yod (י) interchanges with vav (ו)

NOT!

Jastrow - 155 - b.h. - בָּחַן - bauchan
 - to distinguish, examine, to try, to probe, to find out

⑤

Sitting In Judgement Without Distinguishing Or Examining Or Finding Out And Banking The Money

⑥

SAMPLE OF THE HEBREW 'WORD ANALYSIS'

FIGURE II - 1

The Hebrew 'word analysis' though quite simple to use was not acquired quickly but developed during the course of this study. The 'analysis' was used on seventy six names of places taken from modern maps and that led to the patterns of settlement of the abducted people.

The lists of definitions shown in FIGURES II-2- A&B and II-3-A&B are the patterns arising from the data derived from using the Hebrew 'word analysis' as an instrument to convert the names of the modern places to the verbal data shown.

One pattern seen by following the names of the cities shown in blue in FIGURE II-5, the PLACEMENT OF HEBREW 'WORD ANALYSIS' LOCATIONS' reveals what seemed like a forced march east from Mosul in modern day Iraq to Resht on the southern shore of the Caspian Sea, in modern day Iran, and then on to the western part of modern day China.

Another pattern seen by following the names of the cities shown in blue in FIGURE II-5 reveals a possible second forced trip, by land and then by sea west from the southern shore of the Caspian Sea through the Caucasus and the Black Sea to Odesa in what is now Ukraine; and a third pattern seen from following the names of the cities shown in blue in FIGURE II-5 shows possible forced sea trips from Resht on the southern shore of the Caspian Sea north to establish the settlements of Baku, Astrakhan, Guryev and a settlement that was eventually named Krasnovodsk along the western, northern and eastern shores of the Caspian Sea.

When the Assyrians abducted the Samarians they took only 'skilled' people; and the question arises as to what those skills were. Certainly they would have needed the skills of farming, carpentry, smithing, medicine and government; but above all if the Assyrians were to establish the trade route that appears to be developing from the patterns, they would have needed merchants and traders. The merchants and traders whom they would have needed to establish the Trade Route. Looking at the people of Israel we see that the Land of Israel has always been at the cross roads of the East. When Moses led the Children of Israel out of Egypt destined for the promised land The Children of Israel entered the Land of Canaan, the land of milk and honey. The milk and honey wasn't necessarily in the land; the milk and honey could very well have been in the trade. The name Canaan in the language of the Canaanites means merchant. When King Solomon built his fortified cities, he built them around the ports on the Mediterranean Sea and along a line from those ports to the port of Ezion Geber at the head of the Red Sea. It appears that he built those fortified cities not to protect people but to protect the goods, the merchandise. When the Assyrians perpetrated their campaigns of abduction, the first campaign was along a narrow strip of land down the Mediterranean coast taking in all of the port cities and their environs: Acre, Dor, Jaffa, Ashdod and Ashkelon. It appears as though they were after the people who were in trade.

What this study will show is that the Assyrians and their probable Scythian allies were establishing an east-west trade route in the secure, virtually uninhabited lands of present day Central Asia using their captives, the people of 'The Ten Lost Tribes Of Israel', as the 'operators' of the Trade Route to provide layover stops for caravans of traders, and probably to act as the traders themselves.

A fourth pattern of cities' names shown orange colored in FIGURE II-5, shows settlements' names which had most likely developed over a period of time after the first settlements, names which reflected what was done in those more matured towns, like advertisements. Since the Scythian Empire appeared to have reached to the western part of modern day China, it also appears as though those settlements beyond that eastern boundary were settled by later period Samarians or Samarian Descendants.

When the Samarian People were originally abducted from Samaria, they appear to have been brought to an internment camp which according to this study they named Mosul because the definition of the name Mosul would have meant that they had already been tried and convicted without distinguishing or examining or finding out about the people, for no cause, and then their money was taken from them and 'banked'. When people are first put into prison in modern times, their money is often taken from them and 'banked'. The Assyrians apparently didn't want to hurt the people, and wanted to use them for their own purposes of

14

establishing an east-west trade route and it could be suspected that they, the Assyrians, would have used the money to help feed and transport the Samarian People on their way to the sites of their intended settlements along the Trade Route. Looking at a chart showing the demography of the Hebrew People throughout history in Barnavi's book, Reference 2, it could be interpolated as to how many people would have been taken, and the best that this author could estimate was that about 250,000 people over the five year period of the four campaigns were taken.

With the first three campaigns lasting a year each and the last campaign lasting two years, this estimate of 250,000 people when divided into approximately 50,000 people a year, and considering annual ten month campaigns, results in about 5,000 people a month, and roughly 1250 people a week being taken. In a six day week then, roughly 200-250 people a day would have been processed through Mosul. If the people were broken down into family groups of about twenty persons per family group, the Assyrians would have to deal with only about ten people, the ten family leaders of the 200-250 people per day going out of Mosul, which should have been handleable. Considering that people would need only about a pound and a half of water and a quarter pound of meat a day to sustain themselves, and that the Scythians, who would have provided the logistics along the trails, were nomadic herders, it is conceivable for them to have provided the food, and again, perhaps using the money taken from the Samarians in Mosul to pay for it. The Scythians could have had cattle or other livestock waiting for the people at the various settlements and sites along the trails, which would most certainly had to have had water supplies. The twenty people in each family group most likely would have required a total of about 300 pounds of water and 50 pounds of meat for the ten day trek between settlements and sites, with one or two horses being required to carry the food and water supply for each family. This is all conceivable in a logistical situation and would require the Assyrians or Scythians to butcher cattle or other livestock for only fifty pounds of meat a day at each settlement or site for the traveling people. This would have been an intensive operation but a conceivable one; and since the cost of the food and the other costs would most likely have come from the 'banked money' in Mosul, the abducted Samarian People would have been paying for their own food and transportation.

A means of hiding the existence of the Trade Route from the 'world' over the next century and a half and after the 597 B.C.E. Babylonian exile of Judeans and probable start up of contact of those Judeans with the Samarian Traders' Descendants from potential robbers, it can be suspected that 'stories' would have been passed to hide what had happened to the Samarians. For instance, one story that appeared over the centuries as to what happened to them was that they were taken beyond the Sambatyon River over which Jews are not allowed to pass. In fact, Mosul is on the western bank of the Tigris River, a boundary which in ancient times may well have been the eastern 'end of the world' for the Hebrews. Perhaps other meanings can be read into 'the Sambatyon River over which Jews are not allowed to pass'.

FIGURE II-2-A is a list of names of original settlements given to them by the Samarian Settlers. The names indicate the affects of the long and hard journeys on the people and what the people had to have felt when reaching these sites of their new homes for what would probably have to be a long time.

FIGURE II-2-A

LIST OF DEFINED IN ENGLISH NAMES OF ORIGINAL SETTLEMENTS

1. Mosul – City in the nation of Iraq
– 'Sitting In Judgement Without Distinguishing Or Examining Or Finding Out And Banking The Money'

2. Resht – City in the nation of Iran
– 'It Is Indeed Dispossessed And In Poverty'

3. Ashkhabad – City in the nation of Turkmenistan
'Having Large Testicles Alone'

4. Kara Kum Desert – In the nation of Turkmenistan
– 'Cut (By) The Heat Not A Dark Place To Hide'

5. Khiva – City in the nation of Turkmenistan
– 'Border'

6. **Bukhara – City in the nation of Uzbekistan**
    – 'Selected'

7. **Alay Mountain Range – In the nations of Uzbekistan, Tajikistan and Kyrgyzstan**
    – 'Above And About Me'

8. **Yovan – City in the nation of Tajikistan**
    – 'Parched And Dry To Build For Whom'

9. **Kashgar – City in the nation of China**
    – 'The Difficulty Has Diminished, No (More) Grief'

10. **Yarkand – City in the nation of China**
    – 'Saw Green, Went Down, Took Possession And Built'

11. **Alma Ata – City in the nation of Kazakhstan**
    – 'To Conceal And Cover Ourselves'

12. **Balkhash and Lake Balkhash – City and lake in the nation of Kazakhstan**
    – 'Worn Out And Affected By Pain Not He'

13. **Bet Pak Dalc – Desert region in the nation of Kazakhstan**
    – 'The Household Here Is A Sparse Pit'

14. Karazhal – City in the nation of Kazakhstan
   – 'Kneel In The Running Waters'

15. Karaganda – City in the nation of Kazakhstan
   – 'Languish On Bended Knee In Garden
   Without Dark Clouds'

16. Pavlodar – City in the nation of Kazakhstan
   – 'Here, Lod (Is To Be The) Distinguished Leader'

17. Zaysan – City in the nation of China
   – 'To Erect The Symbol Of The Leaf Of The Palm
   Tree And Not Break It'

18. Ayaguz – City in the nation of Kazakhstan
   – 'Past The Fortified Town Not To See (It)'

19. Novosibirsk – City in the nation of Russia
   – 'To Spring Forth Hope'

20. Turan – City in the nation of Russia
   – 'I Pray Not (To Be) Upon The Mountain'

21. Solun – City in the nation of China
   – 'It Is Indeed (To) Ascend'

22. Azerbaijan – The nation of Azerbaijan
– 'To Strengthen In Entering This Kind Of
Native Citizenry Without Uniting'

**23. Azerbaidzhan – The nation of Azerbaijan in a different spelling
from the previous one**
– 'To Girdle (Ourselves) In Breaking Into
The Native Citizenry (Which Is)
Offensive, Without Firmness, Strength Or
Power'

24. Ganca – City in the nation of Azerbaijan
– 'Garden Here'

25. Armenia – The nation of Armenia
– 'The Palace Arom, Half Done'

26. Georgia – The nation of Georgia
– 'Redeemed From The Soft Powerful Trembling'

27. Vani – City in the nation of Georgia
– 'Is It Indeed So Humble And Poor?'

28. Alagir – City in the nation of Georgia
– 'To Arrive And Shout But Not To Live By
Shouting'

29. Armavir – City in the nation of Russia
– 'A Spiced, Sweet And Pleasing Palace, But Not Handsome (Like In) Arom'

30. Rostov – City in the nation of Russia
– 'The Head Is Good To Be'

31. Odesa – City in the nation of Ukraine
– 'Moist, Soppy Cloud Not Becoming'

32. Apseron Peninsula – In the nation of Azerbaijan
– 'Low Spirited And Weary, Nevertheless We Pray'

33. Baku – City in the nation of Azerbaijan
– 'Chosen'

34. Astrakhan – City in the nation of Russia
– '(Under This) Bright Star Take Possession And Build!'

35. Guryev – City in the nation of Kazakhstan
– 'To Lament The Price Of Redemption Without Dark Clouds'

FIGURE II-2-B
DEVELOPMENT OF ENGLISH DEFINITIONS OF NAMES OF ORIGINAL SETTLEMENTS

The abducted Samarian People appear to have been brought to a temporary internment camp which they named Mosul meaning that they had already been tried and convicted for no cause, and then their money was taken and 'banked'.

1. Mosul – City in the nation of Iraq

Jastrow - 751 - b.h.- מוֹשָׁב - moshauv
- seat, sitting (in judgement)

Jastrow - 1534 - b.h. - שׁוּלְחָנִי - shoolkhaunee
- money changer, banker

מוֹשָׁב שׁוּלְחָנִי

מוֹשׁוּל - Mosul

Jastrow - 559- yod(י) interchanges with vav(ו)
NOT!
Jastrow - 155 - b.h.- בַּחַן - bauchan
- to distinguish, examine, to try, to probe, to find out

Sitting In Judgement Without Distinguishing Or Examining Or Finding Out And Banking The Money

----

Visualizing the Samarian People as having been torn from their homes on or near the Mediterranean coast of Israel, from the port cities, from their farms on the coastal plains and from their shops it is easy to see that they were dispossessed. They were marched into an internment camp where their money was taken from them so they had to have felt more dispossessed. After the first of them were marched through the desert and mountains to the end of their known world, the south shore of the Caspian Sea, and were told that this was where they were to live forever, the veil of despair coming from their dispossession would have enveloped them and that is what they named their settlement, Resh, which when translated from Biblical Hebrew to English means dispossessed. The name Resht coming from the post Biblical Hebrew word, raushoot, had to have come later, after the establishment of the settlements when the Trade Route grew prosperous further north through the ports of Baku on the western and Krasnovodsk on the eastern shores of the Caspian Sea. The word raushoot, meaning poverty, is the only word in the 'blue' settlements of FIGURE II-5, the original settlements, bearing a post Biblical Hebrew root. All of the other names have exclusively Biblical Hebrew root words. The names of the 'orange' settlements in FIGURE II-5 have mixtures of Biblical and post Biblical Hebrew root words, but those 'orange' settlements also have predominately Biblical Hebrew root words with the post Biblical Hebrew root words appearing to have come in the post Babylonian exile period from 597 B.C.E. onward when Judeans became involved with the Samarians and their descendants on the Trade Route. The original settlement name can be suspected to have been Resh.

2. Resht – City in the nation of Iran

Jastrow - 1498 - b.h. - רֵשׁ - resh
- dispossessed, poor

Jastrow - 1499 - p.b.h. - רָשׁוּת - raushoot
- poverty

רֵשׁ רָשׁוּת

רֵשׁת - Resht

NOT!
Jastrow - 371 - ו - vav
- is it indeed so!

A 'NOT!' 'is it indeed so?' is a strong 'it is indeed so!'.

It Is Indeed Dispossessed And In Poverty

Where the desert meets the mountains, which is a very difficult place to live, where people had to have been courageous, strong and tough to survive is the site that the people who settled there named Ashkhabad.

3. Ashkhabad – City in the nation of Turkmenistan

Jastrow - 128 - b.h. - אֶשֶׁךְ - eshek
- one having large testicles

Jastrow - 139 - b.h. - בַּד - bad
- alone, apart

אֶשֶׁךְ בַּד
| \ / / /
אֶשׁכבד - Ashkhabad

Having Large Testicles Alone

In the middle of the desert the heat was all around and the people had no place to hide from it. They had very little to sense but the heat, most likely overbearing. This was the Kara Kum Desert.

4. Kara Kum Desert – In the nation of Turkmenistan

Jastrow - 674 - b.h. - כָּרַת - kaurat
- to cut

Jastrow - 435 - b.h. - חוֹם - khoom
- summer, heat

כָּרַת חוֹם
| \ \ / /
כָּר קוֹם - Kara Kum

25

NOT!

Jastrow - 1641 - b.h. - תָּא - tau - cell [implies being
hidden in dark place]

Cut (By) The Heat Not A Dark Place To Hide

Security was also an issue for the new settlers, with some places being more dangerous to live than others. The settlement of Khiva probably had more to fear from the surroundings than others and so was apparently fortified.

5. Khiva – City in the nation of Turkmenistan

Jastrow - 490 - b.h. - חַף - khauf
- border, shore

חַף

ן ו

חַב - Khiva

Jastrow - 134 - vav (ב) interchanges with peh (פ, ף)

Border

Sometimes a site would have been plainly acceptable to the people so they were apparently more nonchalant about naming it, such as in the case of Bukhara.

26

6. Bukhara – City in the nation of Uzbekistan

Jastrow - 155 - b.h. - בָּחַר - baukhar
- to try examine, to
choose, select, prefer

בָּחר
| | |
בָּחַר - Bukhara

Selected

The Alay Mountain Range, the first Hebraic sounding place to have been struck in this study will remain the favorite.

7. Alay Mountain Range – In the nations of Uzbekistan, Tajikistan and Kyrgyzstan

Jastrow - 1080 - b.h. - עַל - al
- height, upon, above,
about me

עַל
| |
עַל - Alay

Above And About Me

Unlike Bukhara, some sites were less than a questionable choice for settlement and the people named them accordingly as in the case of Yovan, built in a mountainous desert region.

8. Yovan – City in the nation of Tajikistan

Jastrow - 562 - b.h. - יָבֵשׁ - yauvaesh
-parched, dry, to wither

Jastrow - 176 - b.h. - בני - vnae
- to build

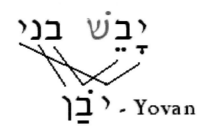

יָבֵשׁ בני

יָבֵן - Yovan

NOT!
Jastrow - 1505 - b.h. - שׁ' - sheen
- prefix for: who, which, that, for

A 'NOT!' prefix is a suffix.

Parched And Dry To Build For Whom

Kashgar seems to be in a valley between high mountains.

9. Kashgar – City in the nation of China

Jastrow - 1429 - b.h. - קָשֶׁה - kaushe
- stiff, hard, difficult

Jastrow - 271 - b.h. - גְּרַע - gaura
- to diminish, deduct

קָשֶׁה גְּרַע

קַשְׁגַּר - Kashgar

Jastrow - 1034 - ayeen (ע) interchanges with heh (ה)
NOT!
Jastrow - 335 - b.h. - הָה - hau
- ah, alas

The Difficulty Has Diminished, No (More) Grief

The Samarian settlers had apparently been traveling in the mountains and then descended into a fertile valley to establish their settlement, Yarkand, which is a city on a river of the same name in a flat region below the Pamir Mountain Range.

10. Yarkand – City in the nation of China

Jastrow - 597 - b.h. - יֶרֶק - yerek
- green, herb

Jastrow - 594 - b.h. - יָרֶד - yauraed
- to go down, to enter, to leave

Jastrow - 1391 - b.h. - קָנָה - kaunau
- establish, to create, acquire, own, take possession

Jastrow - 1393 - b.h. - קָנֶן - kaunaen
- to put up, build

יֶרֶק יָרֶד קָנָה קָנֶן

יַרְקַנְד - Yarkand

NOT!

Jastrow - 327 - b.h. - ה - heh
- an interrogative prefix

A 'NOT!' interrogative prefix could be an exclamation point.

Saw Green, Went Down, Took Possession And Built!

Whereas Kashgar and Yarkand are in valleys Alma Ata is in the Tien Shan Mountains, a continuation of the Alay Mountain Range. Apparently the people of Alma Ata needed to conceal themselves in the mountains as differing from those of Kashgar and Yarkand who appeared to have been secure in their valleys.

11. Alma Ata – City in the nation of Kazakhstan

Jastrow - 1084 - b.h. - עָלַם - aulam
- to surround, to tie up, to conceal

Jastrow - 1063 - b.h. - עָטָה - autau
- to wrap up, to cover oneself

עָטָה עָלַם

עָטָה עָלֵם - Alma Ata

To Conceal And Cover Ourselves

Balkhash and Lake Balkhash are at the foot of the Alay Mountain Range through which the Samarian Settlers had to have traveled to get to the Lake Balkhash settlements. From the definition of the name Balkhash the trip had to have been arduous but the people were not daunted.

12. Balkhash and Lake Balkhash – City and lake in the nation of Kazakhstan

Jastrow - 172 - b.h. - בָּלָה - baulau
- crumbled, to be worn out, to fail, decay, perish

Jastrow - 441 - b.h. - חוּשׁ - khoosh
- to feel, to feel pain, be affected

בָּלָה חוּשׁ

בַּלְקָשׁ - Balkash

NOT!

Jastrow - 335 - הוּ = הוּא - hoo = hoo

Jastrow - 335 - b.h. - הוּא - hoo
- he

Worn Out And Affected By Pain Not He

Bet Pak Dalc is a mountainous desert region of the Kazakh Hills. It is conceivable that the Bet could have originally been Bayit with the vowels replaced with time leading to Bet and so eliminating the post Biblical Hebrew reference and the extraneous word 'Here' in the definition.

13. Bet Pak Dalc – Desert region in the nation of Kazakhstan

Jastrow - 167 - b.h. - בַּיִת - bayit
- house, household, home

Jastrow - 1154 - b.h. - פַחַת - pakhat
- cavity, pit

Jastrow - 308 - b.h. - דַל - dal
- thin, sparse, poor, needy

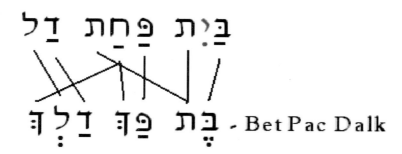

בַּיִת פַחַת דַל

בֵּת פַּק דַלְךְ - Bet Pac Dalk

NOT!
Jastrow - 559 - p.b.h. - אֵי - yae
- where?

A 'NOT!' 'where?' is a 'here'.

The Household Here Is A Sparse Pit

Karazhal, in the Kazakh Hills of Kazakhstan, had to have had a stream or brook flowing through the site designated for settlement by virtue of the name given it.

14. Karazhal – City in the nation of Kazakhstan

Jastrow - 672 - b.h. - כָּרַע - kaura
- bow, bend the knee

Jastrow - 390 - b.h. - זָהַל - zauhal
- flow, running waters

כָּרַע זָהַל

כָּרַזְהל - Karazhal

Kneel In The Running Waters

Karaganda appears to be in a valley of the Bet Pak Dalc Region of the Kazakh Hills of Kazakhstan. Modern agricultural products include grains. In the vernacular of the Samarian People a 'gan' could be considered a good place to live and grow agricultural products; and dark clouds, which could bring rain, connote blessings; but here there appeared to have been no blessings, no matter how good a place it was to live. The people were not happy.

34

15. Karaganda – City in the nation of Kazakhstan

Jastrow - 672 - b.h. - כָּרַע - kaura
- bow, bend the knee

Jastrow - 256 - b.h. - גַּן - gan
- fenced in place, garden

Jastrow - 275 - b.h. - דָאַב - dauav
- languish

כָּרַע גַּן דָאַב

כָּרְגַּנְד - Karaganda

NOT!

Jastrow - 1034 - b.h. - עָב - auv
- thick dark clouds

Languish On Bended Knee In Garden Without Dark Clouds

Pavlodar is on the Irtysh River where modern agricultural products include grains and where settlers must have recognized the fact that the land would be productive as it was in their home city of Lod.

16. Pavlodar – City in the nation of Kazakhstan

Jastrow - 1131 - b.h. - פְּאֵר - p'aer
- to cut off, to distinguish, ornament, crown, bonnet of distinction

Jastrow - 694 - b.h. - לוֹד - lod - Lydda, Lod, a city one day west of Jerusalem [on a modern map. Lod, Lydda, is about 25 miles northwest of Jerusalem]

Jastrow - 320 - b.h. - דָּרְבָן - daurvaun
- leader, the iron point on the staff,

פְּאֵר לוֹד דָּרְבָן

פַּוְלָדָר -Pavlodar

NOT!

Jastrow - 80 - b.h. - אָן - aun
- where?

A 'NOT!' 'where?' is a 'here', so the word, 'Here', is added.

Here, Lod (Is To Be The) Distinguished Leader

36

Zaysan is in a valley within the Altay Mountain Range at the headwaters of the Irtysh River.

17. Zaysan – City and lake in the nation of Kazakhstan

Jastrow - 409 - b.h. - זָקַף - zaukaf
- to join, put together, erect, restore

Jastrow - 400 - b.h. - זֵכֶר - zaekher
- memorial, remembrance, symbol

Jastrow - 1008 - b.h. - סַנְסִן - sansan
- prick, leaf of the palm tree

זָקַף זֵכֶר סַנְסִן

זֵסַן - Zaysan

NOT!

Jastrow - 1238 - b.h. - פָרַק - paurak
- to break, separate, to untie, loosen

To Erect The Symbol Of The Leaf Of The Palm Tree And Not Break It

Ayaguz appears to be in a valley of the Altay Mountain Range on a river feeding Lake Balkhash established beyond an already existing fortified town.

18. Ayaguz – City in the nation of Kazakhstan

Jastrow - 1075 - b.h. - עִיר - eer
  - watchtower, fort, town, city

Jastrow - 220 - b.h. - גוּז - gooz
  - To cut, pass, fly, to carry across, drive up, to cross

עִיר   גוּז

\\\|//

עִיגוּז - Ayaguz

NOT!

Jastrow - 1435 - b.h. - רְאִי - r'au
  - to see

Past The Fortified Town Not To See (It)

38

Novosibirsk is on the Ob River in the foothills of the Altay and Sayan Mountain Ranges. It is seemingly named after Nob, a city in the tribal area of Benjamin; and although the tribal areas of Benjamin went to the Kingdom of Judah after the eventual division of the Kingdom of David and Solomon, it is conceivable that members of the Tribe of Benjamin may have been living on land going to the Kingdom of Samaria. The tsadee koof (צק) part of the name Novosibirsk could have been in the vernacular of the Samarian People to symbolize a plague like disaster since the expression could have been based on the Biblical plagues used to effect the Exodus from Egypt. It could perhaps not have appeared in the Hebrew Bible as such and therefor not in the Midrashic works used by Professor Jastrow for the Biblical words used in his dictionary, but appeared in the Talmudic writings giving it the post Biblical Hebrew notation shown below. The application of the tsadee koof (צק) could have been made in much later times when perhaps that town as well as many other towns and villages throughout Russia were beset by some terrible misgiving. Then this town and others like it would have taken up the 'plague' terminology. A value judgement brings this explanation to the fore, and so the original name would have been, Novosibir, 'To Spring Forth Hope'.

19. Novosibirsk – City in the nation of Russia

Jastrow - 883 - b.h. - נוֹב - noov
- to spring forth, to flow

Jastrow - 952 - b.h. - סֶבֶר - sever
- hope

Jastrow - 317 - p.b.h. - צָד - tsk
- the first letters of the
names of the second and
third plagues on Egypt

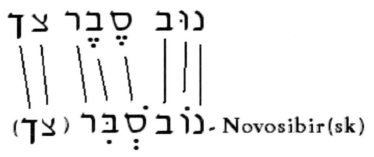

נֹוב סֶבְּר צָד

(צָד) נֹוב סִבְּר - Novosibir(sk)

To Spring Forth Hope

Turan is in the Sayan Mountains.

20. Turan – City in the nation of Russia

Jastrow - 526 - b.h. - טוּרָא - toorau
- mount, mountain

Jastrow - 865 - b.h. - נָא - nau
- I pray

טוּרָא נָא

טוּרַן - Turan

NOT!
Jastrow - 1 - א - alef
- upon, over (as a prefix)

I Pray Not (To Be) Upon The Mountain

Solun is on a river on the eastern side of the Great Khingan Mountain Range. It appears as if the settlers may have ascended into the mountains from the river but remained close to it. The settlement, and now the city appears to be in the heights overlooking the river. Although the name Solun represents the feelings of a people undergoing a hard trek, this author believes that it was settled some time after the original settlements because it exists in a region not controlled by the Scythians at the time of the founding of the original settlements. It may well have been settled by people moving east out of the Scythians' territories to form the peoples whom we now know as the Mongols.

21. Solun – City in the nation of China

Jastrow - 964 - b.h. - סוּלָם - soolaum
- ascent, ladder

סוּלָם

\| i̇ /

סֻלָן - Solun

NOT!
Jastrow - 371 - ו - vav
- is it indeed so?

A 'NOT!' 'is it indeed so?' is a strong 'it is indeed so!'.

It Is Indeed (To) Ascend

During the third campaign of abduction the Assyrians went east to the Kingdom of Arom taking people from, most likely, the tribes of Simon and Reuben. Whereas those tribes of Simon and Reuben were originally settled in the southern part of the Land of Israel, they had to have moved north above the boundary shown in FIGURE I-4 prior to the abductions in order to have been abducted by the Assyrians. Otherwise they would have remained with the Kingdom of Judah and would have been spared abduction; and then there would have been only eight lost tribes of Israel. A likely place for them to have resettled from the desert of southern Israel was to the fertile land near Damascus during the Kingdom of David and Solomon. In any case those people living in Arom near Damascus were resettled into the western arm of the Trade Route by the Assyrians and probably the Scythians, into the Caucasus and further west to present day Ukraine. Unlike the eastern arm of the Trade Route which was mostly uninhabited desert and mountain areas, this western arm appeared to

42

have been settled into more populated areas, areas better suited for habitation.

22. Azerbaijan – The nation of Azerbaijan

Jastrow - 38 - b.h. - אָזַר - auzar
  - to put around, girdle, strengthen

Jastrow - 159 - b.h. - בִּיאָח - beeaukh
  - coming in, entrance

Jastrow - 38 - b.h. - אֶזְרָח - ezraukh
  - planted, native, citizen

Jastrow - 405 - b.h. - זַן - zan
  - kind, species

אֶזְרָח בִּיאָח אָזַר זַן

אָזֶרְבִּיזַן - Azerbaijan

NOT!
Jastrow - 40 - b.h. - אָחָח - aukhaukh
  - to unite

To Strengthen In Entering This Kind Of Native Citizenry Without Uniting

----

It appears that in the spellings of Azerbaijan and Azerbaidzhan that a slight difference in consonant spellings brings forth only a slight difference in the English definitions.

23. Azerbaidzhan – The nation of Azerbaijan in a spelling different from that of the previous one.

Jastrow - 38 - b.h. - אָזַר - auzar
- to put around, girdle, strengthen

Jastrow - 141 - b.h. - בָּדַק - baudak
- to split, to break into, penetrate

Jastrow - 38 - b.h. - אָזְרָח - ezraukh
- planted, native, citizen

Jastrow - 382 - b.h. - זָהַם - zham
- to be offensive

אָזַר בָּדַק אָזְרָח זָהַם

אָזֶרְבִּידְזָהַן - Azerbaidzhan

NOT!
Jastrow - 628 - b.h. - כֹּחַ - koakh
- firmness, strength, power

To Girdle (Ourselves) In Breaking Into The Native Citizenry (Which Is) Offensive, Without Firmness, Strength Or Power

Ganca appears to be in the only flat, rich, sea level farmland region in the southern Caucasus along the Trade Route; and since a garden was apparently considered a good place to live and grow crops Ganca was an appropriate name for such a settlement.

24. Ganca – In the nation of Azerbaijan

Jastrow - 256 - b.h. - גַן - gan
- garden

Jastrow - 605 - b.h. - כָּא - kau
- here

גַן כָּא

גַנְכָּא - Ganca

Garden Here

Samarian settlers of what is now modern day Armenia appeared to have come from Arom, which was in what is now modern day Syria where cereal and horticultural crops are grown. These products were apparently similar to those produced in their native Arom making their new settlements very much like their previous homes. However, the people apparently liked Arom better than they did Armenia which is perhaps why they named Armenia, Armenia, 'The Palace Arom, Half Done' or, not quite as good as Arom but like Arom.

25. Armenia – The nation of Armenia

Jastrow - 122 - b.h. - אַרְמוֹן - armon
- enclosure, palace

Jastrow - 122 - b.h. - אַרְמִי - armae
- Syrian, [biblical land of the Arameans]

Jastrow - 865 - b.h. - נָא - nau
- hurried, half done

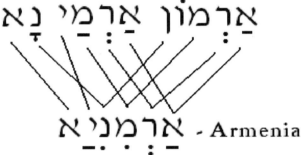

אַרְמוֹן אַרְמִי נָא

אַרְמְנִיָא - Armenia

The Palace Arom, Half Done

The nation of Georgia in the Caucasus has a history of earthquakes which the Samarian Settlers apparently experienced at least once and so they apparently named their settlement for an earthquake.

26. Georgia – The nation of Georgia

Jastrow - 201 - b.h. - גְּאוּלָךְ - g'oolaukh
- redemption, delivery

Jastrow - 1450 - b.h. - רְגַשׁ - regash
- to tremble, shake

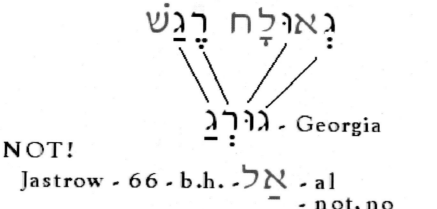

גְּאוּלָח רֶגֶשׁ

גּוּרְגּ - Georgia

NOT!

Jastrow - 66 - b.h. - אַל - al
- not, no

Jastrow - 509 - b.h. - חשׁי - khashi
- to whisper, be
silent, quiet

A 'NOT!' 'not quiet' is possibly a 'soft powerful'.

Redeemed From The Soft Powerful Trembling

Vani is located in the western part of modern day Georgia and although in the western part of the country which was at the time of the abductions linked to Greek influences, Vani appeared to have been founded as a city related to the east, to Assyria and Persia. At the beginning the city was poor but in a short time, within a century, the city turned very wealthy from trade with the Greeks and from the establishment of an extensive iron making industry which presumably traded eastward.

27. Vani – City in the nation of Georgia

Jastrow - 3 71 - b.h. - וַ - va
- is it indeed so?

Jastrow - 1094 - b.h. - עָנִי - auni
- afflicted, humble, poor

עָנִי
\\\\ /
וְעָנִי - Vani

Is It Indeed So Humble And Poor?

With the Assyrians having had two years experience in abducting Samarians they appeared to have established a 'learning curve' which gave rise to an easier transition for the abducted people in entering the new lands. In addition, instead of settling into mountains and deserts as the settlers in the east did, these later abducted Samarians found well established indigenous peoples in the Caucasus, in lands more suitable for human existence and they apparently found these lands to be very much like the lands that they had left in Arom. Putting these factors together, one would expect that these Samarians would have been a lot happier than the Samarians who settled the eastern arm of the Trade Route. So the meaning of 'To Arrive And Shout But Not To Live By Shouting' means, it's fine to be happy, but now it is time to settle down and start making a home for yourselves.

28. Alagir – City in the nation of Georgia

Jastrow - 1081 - b.h. - עָלָה - aulaukh
- to go up, rise, to come up, arrive

Jastrow - 261 - b.h. - גְּעַר - g'ar
- to shout, to rebuke

עָלְגַר - Alagir

NOT!

Jastrow - 415 - b.h. - חָאִי = חיי

Jastrow - 454 - b.h. - חיי - khai
- to live

To Arrive And Shout But Not To Live By Shouting

- - - - - - - - - - - - - - - - -

In Armavir, the Samarians apparently found a place very much like they had in Arom but not quite as nice. Looking at some walled in villages or neighborhoods in modern day northern Iraq, it may be expected that the palaces described here could have resembled those places, small attached homes with large open center spaces all enclosed by mud walls, making the insides of the compounds very intimate and secure.

29. Armavir – City in the nation of Russia

Jastrow - 122 - b.h. - אַרְמוֹן - armon
                             - enclosure, palace

Jastrow - 1110 - b.h. - עָרֵב - aureeve
                             - spiced, sweet, pleasing

Jastrow - 122 - b.h. - אַרְמִי - armae
                             - Syrian, [biblical land
                               of the Arameans]

אַרְמְבר - Armavir

Jastrow - 1034 - ayeen (ע) interchanges with alef (א)

Jastrow - 559 - yod (י) interchanges with vav (ו)

NOT!
Jastrow - 866 - b.h. - נָאִי - nae
                             - to be becoming, handsome

A Spiced, Sweet And Pleasing Palace, But Not Handsome (Like In) Arom

----

Rostov is at the mouth of the Don River which is at the head of the Sea of Azov and is the most northerly part of the Black Sea. The land is basically at sea level with modern crops being wheat and corn; a region that was a good place to grow things. With the river, the settlers had a lot of water and trade with the northern indigenous peoples and so Rostov was a good place to be.

30. Rostov – City in the nation of Russia

Jastrow - 1437 - b.h. - רֹאשׁ - rosh

- head point, beginning, heading, main thing, principal

Jastrow - 521 - b.h. - טוֹב - tov

- to be good, fit, valuable

רֹאשׁ טוֹב

/ / / | / / |

רֹאשׁ טוֹב - Rostov

The Head Is Good To Be

Odesa is on the Black Sea at the mouth of the Dniester River just north of the mouth of the Danube and just east of the mouth of the Dnieper River with all three rivers emptying into the Black Sea between fifty and one hundred miles of Odesa. The Samarian People coming from the dry atmosphere of Israel were not accustomed to the kind of humidity that they encountered on the north western shore of the Black Sea and had to have found all of that humidity disagreeable; and what they felt is what they named their settlement, Odesa, 'Moist, Soppy Cloud Not Becoming'.

51

31. Odesa – City in the nation of Ukraine

Jastrow - 15 - b.h. - אֵד - aed
- vapor, cloud

Jastrow - 326 - b.h. - דָּשֵׁן - daushain
- to be moist, soppy

אֵד דָּשֵׁן

אֹדֶשׁ - Odesa

NOT!
Jastrow - 866 - b.h. - נְאִי - nauy
- to be becoming

Moist, Soppy Cloud Not Becoming

The next four settlements seemed to have been settled by people coming from the Tribe of Ephraim in the final campaign of the Assyrian abductions. These people lived inland from the Mediterranean coast and were apparently unaccustomed to seeing or being on large bodies of water. After having gone through the abduction, the march to the internment camp and the march to the seacoast settlement of Resh(t); and then being taken on what may well have been a frightening boat trip up the Caspian Sea, one would expect them to have been low spirited and weary and this is what they named their first sign of land, the Apseron Peninsula.

32. Apseron Peninsula – In the nation of Azerbaijan

Jastrow - 99 - b.h. - אַף - af
- also, too, the same, breath, nose, face, cheeks, weariness, nevertheless

Jastrow - 1021 - b.h. - סָר - saur
- one whom courage has left, low spirited

Jastrow - 80 - b.h. - אָן - an
- where, oh!, I pray

אָן סָר אַף

אַפְסָרָן - Apseron

Low Spirited And Weary, Nevertheless We Pray

After the people who had sailed partly up the Caspian Sea disembarked from their boat(s) onto land, which was at sea level, perhaps they found the land to be similar to their homeland in southern Samaria. In any case they apparently liked the land and named it, 'Chosen'. Perhaps they also saw the oil oozing from the Earth and saw better times coming.

33. Baku – City in the nation of Azerbaijan

Jastrow - 154 - b.h. - בָּחוּר - baukhoor
- chosen

בָּחוּר
//
בָּכוּ - Baku

NOT!
Jastrow - 1434 - b.h. - ר - resh - is used as a formative
letter at the end of a
word and so can be
dropped

Chosen

The next group of people also most likely from the Tribe of Ephraim sailed to the northern most reaches of the Caspian Sea. Perhaps navigating by the stars, they sailed a short distance up into the Volga River and were apparently enthusiastic about the site that they found because they named their settlement, 'Under This Bright Star Take Possession And Build'.

34. Astrakhan – City in the nation of Russia

Jastrow - 99 - b.h. - אֶסְתֵּר - Estaer
- bright star

Jastrow - 1391 - b.h. - קָנָה - kaunau
- to establish, to create,
to acquire, own, to take
possession

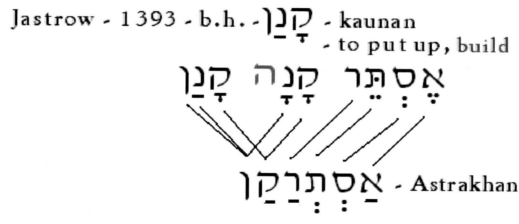

Jastrow - 1393 - b.h. - קָנַן - kaunan
- to put up, build

אֶסְתֵּר קָנָה קָנַן

אַסְתְּרַקֶן - Astrakhan

NOT!
Jastrow - 327 - b.h. - ה - heh
- is it not?

A 'NOT!' 'is it not?' is a double negative and so is a positive with an exclamation point(!).

(Under This) Bright Star Take Possession And Build!

The Caspian Sea settlement at the mouth of the Ural River on the north shore of the Caspian Sea, Guryev, was also likely settled by people from the Tribe of Ephraim; but these people appeared to be not as happy as the people who had settled Baku and Astrakhan. Perhaps they sailed up the Caspian Sea at a time when there may have been rough weather. Whatever their hardships may have been they apparently felt them and gave their settlement the name Guryev meaning, 'To Lament The Price Of Redemption Without Dark Clouds'; 'Without Dark Clouds' meaning without being blessed, where dark clouds relate to rain and rain relates to being blessed. When they landed at the site, at sea level where they could grow wheat and other produce, they were redeemed, they were not at sea any more, but they weren't happy; they didn't feel as though they were blessed.

35. Guryev – City in the nation of Kazakhstan

Jastrow - 271 - b.h. - גָּרַע - gaura
- to scrape off, diminish, deduct, to calculate the price of redemption in proportion to the years served and to be served

Jastrow - 560 - b.h. - יָבַב - yauvav
- to speak in a trembling voice, to lament

גָּרַע יָבַב

| | //

גָּרִיב - Guryev

NOT!

Jastrow - 1034 - b.h. - עָב - auv
- thick, dark clouds

To Lament The Price Of Redemption Without Dark Clouds

56

The original Samarians must have kept close relationships with each other within and between the settlements and then between the villages and towns, so that a support infrastructure of specialties appeared to have developed between the settlements. The names of specialty villages and towns are shown in FIGURE II-3-A while FIGURE II-3-B provides the Hebrew 'word analysis' definitions of those names from Biblical and post Biblical Hebrew. The orange colored definitions are of the settlements and their modern cities' and places' names shown in FIGURE II-5. The burgundy colored definitions in this section are the names of peoples.

FIGURE II-3-A

LIST OF DEFINED IN ENGLISH NAMES OF SETTLEMENTS GIVEN AFTER ESTABLISHMENT OF THE TRADE ROUTE

1. Moldova – The nation of Moldova
   – 'Issues Plenty'

2. Krasnodar – City in the nation of Russia
   – 'Humiliated In The Vow (For) A Merchant's License (From) The Hater (Without Doing) Wrong'

3. Sukhumi – City in the nation of Russia
   – 'To Anoint (With) Wealth'

4. Chechnia – A republic in the nation of Russia
   – 'To Chain And Lock Up Unto'

5. Circassian – A people in the Caucasus and in the nation of Israel
   – 'To Clasp And Hide The Moneybags'

6. Cherkesee – A people in the Caucasus
   – 'To Travel About As A Merchant And Cut Without (The Benefit Of) A Drug'

7. Tbilisi – City in the nation of Georgia
　　　– 'Spice And Ripe Spicy Plants'

8. Tevuz – City in the nation of Azerbaijan
　　　– 'This Is A Grain Harvest!'

9. Yerevan – City in the nation of Armenia
　　　– 'Shaking In Multitudes And Trembling In Fear,
　　　We Pray (With) No Desires'

10. Mt. Ararat – Mountain in the nation of Turkey
　　　– 'In Awe Of The Mountain'

11 Sumqayit – City in the nation of Azerbaijan
　　　– 'To Pack And Join (For The) Summer'

12. Tabriz – City in the nation of Iran
　　　– 'Pure Iron, Free Of Coals Or Ashes And Not
　　　Blackened Or Charred Unto'

13. Kazanka – City in the nation of Kazakhstan
　　　– 'The Giant In Anger Cuts Down Like God
　　　Without A Drug Or A Crowd Of People'

14. Krasnovodsk – City in the nation of Turkmenistan
　　　– 'Certain To Spring Forth A Tax On The
　　　Bags Of Produce Here'

15. Nebit Dag – City in the nation of Turkmenistan
　　　– 'Nebat – The Military Police Barracks Unto'

16. Kazandzhik – City in the nation of Turkmenistan
　　　– 'The Falsehood (Of The) State Officials,
　　　Without A Woe, Not The Father'

17. Gorgan – City in the nation of Iran
　　　– 'The Flour Wheel Worked With The Pressure
　　　Of Water (But) Not (By) Scholars'

18. Kizyl Arvat – City in the nation of Turkmenistan
– 'The Servant Girls Certainly Wait And Howl In The Desert'

19. Samarkand – City in the nation of Uzbekistan
– 'Drugs And Druggist's Preparations, (Made From) The Rounded Off Seed Grain Without The Upper Portion, (That Make One) Feel Comfortable Without Being Lost Or Going Astray'

20. Kabul – City in the nation of Afghanistan
– 'To Receive A Stolen Measure Prohibited (By Law)'

21. Pamir – Mountain Range in Tajikistan
– 'To Separate, Divide And Exchange Not In The Winding Pathways'

22. Khorog – City in the nation of Tajikistan
– 'It Is Indeed To Meet With And Have Affection For Scholars Who Are Habitual Visitors Of Drinking (Or Smoking) Houses Unto No Measure'

23. Ulan Ude – City in the nation of Russia
– 'Opposite The Thick Dark Red Clay That Does Not (Need) Crushing'

24. Hindu Kush – Region in Kashmir, India, Pakistan and Afghanistan
'To Be Affected (By Those Who Are) Beholden To Be Devoted But Not To Agree With'

25. Tashkent – City in the nation of Uzbekistan
– 'To Arrive And Rest In A Cell Not In The Woods'

26. Tselinograd (Akmolinsk) – City in the nation of Kazakhstan
– 'To Make A Path To Carry Along To Who Scrape And Saw'

27. Akmolinsk (Tselinograd) – City in the nation of Kazakhstan
– 'There Is No Distress In The Amount Of Food To Eat'

28. Novokuznetsk – City in the nation of Russia
– 'The Town That Sprang Forth In Growth (Like) Nov Is Dried Up Cannot Sustain Life (So) We Wander For Water'

29. Ubsa Nor – City in the nation of Mongolia
– 'To Fatten And Feed (Livestock Near) The Ploughed Ground'

30. Irkutsk – City in the nation of Russia
– '(Those Who Are) Frightened To Squeeze Through With The Horses Will Not Go Forth'

31. Ulan Batur – City in the nation of Mongolia
– 'To Stay Overnight In Front Of The Mountain (For A) Fee, (Have A) Bath, Not Be Bent Or Tired (And Show) Bad Manners (With) An Untouched Virgin Girl'

32. Sukhe Bator – City in the nation of Russia
– '(Near) The Mountain A Traveler, (For A) Fee, Can Be Washed In A Bath, Have Oils Poured On Him, Show Bad Manners With An Untouched Virgin Girl And Not (Be)'

33. Sukh Batar – Region in the nation of Mongolia
 – '(Near) The Mountain A Traveler, (For A) Fee, Can Be Washed In A Bath, Have Oils Poured On Him, Show Bad Manners With An Untouched Virgin Girl And Not (Be) Pointed (At) And Talk And Tell (Of His Travels)'

34. Uniket – City in the nation of China
 – 'To Possess Wealth By Digging Without Grief'

35. Khana Abasa – City in the nation of China
 – 'To Encamp And Feed'

36. Kirin – City in the nation of China
 – 'A Surrounding Enclosure (For) Protection Not To Burst Forth (Merchandise)'

37. Lupeh – City in the nation of China
 – 'The Steady Torch Without Wood (In The Desert) To Stay Overnight And Redeem And Divide'

38. Ulanhot – City in the nation of China
 – 'Entrance (To Where) The Coals Are Dug'

39. Silinhot – City in the nation of China
 – 'To Ascend In A Path Indeed To The Coals'

40. Huhehot – City in the nation of China
 – 'To Be (In The) Digging Of Coals'

41. Bayinhot – City in the nation of China
 – 'To Move Quickly And Brightly In Search Of The Coal But Not To Burst Forth'

FIGURE II-3-B

DEVELOPMENT OF ENGLISH DEFINITIONS OF NAMES OF SETTLEMENTS GIVEN AFTER ESTABLISHMENT OF THE TRADE ROUTE

Moldova, meaning 'the issuing of plenty', was in trade that the Samarians had with Europe. They moved westward mostly through the rivers to trade and interact with the indigenous peoples whom they found.

1. Moldova – The nation of Moldova

Jastrow - 742 - b.h. - מוֹלָד - molaid
- issue, descendant

Jastrow - 742 - b.h. - מוּלָא - moolau
- plenty, power

מוֹלָד מוּלָא

מוֹלָדֶוָא - Moldova

Issues Plenty

- - - - - - - - - - - - - - - - - -

In Biblical times a vow was a form of donation to the Temple such as a sacrifice or perhaps a fine as a form of repentance; but the giving of a vow for a license was apparently not a part of the Temple agenda, or of the governmental agenda in any of the Kingdoms of Israel. Unaccustomed to such treatment the Samarians and their descendants must have felt angry, but were probably not in a position to act on anger so they felt humiliated and apparently named the licensing offices what they felt, humiliated in having to obtain the licenses for a payment of money. So, Krasnodar was probably a government location and the term hater probably applied to the government.

62

2. Krasnodar – City in the nation of Russia

Jastrow - 672 - b.h. - כָּרַע - kaura
  - saddened, humiliated, subdue, to bow, bend the knee

Jastrow - 1009 - b.h. - סָעַד - sauad
  - to keep off, vow, abstinence

Jastrow - 1005 - p.b.h. - סַנוֹא - sano
  - hater

Jastrow - 322 - b.h. - דְּרוֹר - d'ror
  - amnesty, merchant's license

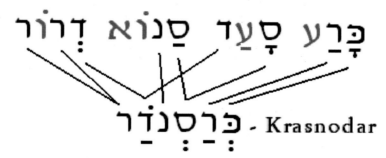

כָּרַע סָעַד סַנוֹא דְּרוֹר

כְּרַסְנָדָר - Krasnodar

Jastrow - 1034 - ayeen (ע) interchanges with alef (א)

NOT!

Jastrow - 1049 - p.b.h. - עָווּ - avauv
  - curve, wrong, iniquity

Humiliated In The Vow (For) A Merchant's License (From)
The Hater (Without Doing) Wrong

- - - - - - - - - - - - - - - - - -

63

Sukhumi is a port city on the eastern coast of the Black Sea. It was to the Black Sea what Krasnovodsk was to the Caspian Sea, a major port tying the Trade Route together. More than Krasnovodsk however, it not only tied Asia to the West, but it tied both Asia and the Middle East to the West. Anyone doing business in Sukhumi would had to have been successful. They would have been anointed with wealth.

3. Sukhumi – City in the nation of Russia

Jastrow - 963 - b.h. - סוּךְ - sook
- boughs, to pour oil, to anoint

Jastrow - 339 - b.h. - הוֹן - hon
- possession, wealth

סוּךְ הוֹן

| \\ / | |

סוּכְהוֹם - Sukhum(i)

Jastrow - 559 - yod (יֹ) interchanges with vav (וֹ)

Jastrow - 721 - mem (מ, ם) interchanges with noon (נ, ן)

To Anoint (With) Wealth

Chechnia's definition in English is 'To Chain And Lock Up Unto', meaning that it contained a prison or bank, but could have been more of a prison, however, because of the chaining statement.

4. Chechnia – A republic in the nation of Russia

Jastrow - 447 - b.h. - חָח - khaukh
  - fasten, clasp, chain

Jastrow - 920 - b.h. - נָעַל - naual
  - to tie (the door), to lock up, close

חָח נָעַל
／／
חֶכְנַיָ - Khekhnia (Chechnia)

NOT!
Jastrow - 685 - b.h. - ל - lamed
  - prefix for unto, to, toward, for

A 'NOT' prefix for unto, to, toward or for is a suffix for unto, to, toward and for.

To Chain And Lock Up Unto

While searching for the name Chechnia in Webster's Hebrew Dictionary, Reference 1, the name Cherkesee was found and defined as a Sunnite Muslim people in the Caucasus, 2,000 of whom settled in Israel's Galilee at about the turn of the Twentieth Century C.E. The people, known for their loyalty to Israel, serve in the country's police and military. Therefore, the name Circassian refers to a people in the modern day Caucasus and in Israel, and appear from the definition to have been money guards in ancient times, perhaps like armored car personnel whom we see in modern times carrying cash from businesses to banks and back.

5. Circassian – A people in Chechnia and the nation of Israel

Jastrow - 1305 - p.b.h. - צְרַר - tsraur
- to be rough, bundle, money-bag

Jastrow - 447 - b.h. - חָח - khaukh
- fasten, clasp, chain

Jastrow - 1292 - b.h. - צָנַע - tsauna
- to hide, to retire

צְרַר חָח צָנַע

סָרְקֶסֵעַן - Circassian

Jastrow - 1256- tsadee (צ) interchanges with samekh (ס)

Jastrow - 415- khet (ח) interchanges with koof (ק)

To Clasp And Hide The Moneybags

The Cherkesee, who appear to also be a people in the modern day Caucasus seem to have been like police, somewhat like the railroad cop of the U.S. depression days and afterward who moved around the Trade Route as railroad police move around the railroad yards and 'beat up all who don't belong there'. The Cherkesees, according to the definition, 'To Travel About As A Merchant And Cut Without (The Benefit Of) A Drug', which apparently means that they would cut people up if they found them stealing. The Cherkesee, then, beat up and mutilated thieves and seemed to have been the protectors of the merchandise. Liberties were taken in using one samekh (ס) for a 'NOT!' definition.

66

6. Cherkesee – A people in Chechnia

Jastrow - 971 - b.h. - סָחַר - saukhar
               - to go around, to travel as a merchant

Jastrow - 1396 - b.h. - קָסַם - kausam
               - to cut, carve, (a curse invoking God as a carver)

סָחַר קָסַם

חֶרְקֵס - Cherkesee

NOT!

Jastrow - 998 - b.h. - סַם - sam
               - drug, medicine, poison

To Travel About As A Merchant And Cut Without (The Benefit Of) A Drug

----

Because of the preponderance of post Biblical Hebrew root words making up the Hebrew 'word analysis' definition of Tbilisi, the city in present day Georgia which apparently became a center for spices, was so named Tbilisi most likely centuries after the first 597 B.C.E. contact with exiled Judeans.

7. Tbilisi – City in the nation of Georgia

Jastrow - 1644 - p.b.h. - תָּבֵל - tevel
 - spice

Jastrow - 715 - p.b.h. - לַפְסָן - lafsen
 - a plant resembling the mustard plant

תָּבֵל לַפְסָן

תְּבִלְס - Tbilisi

NOT!
Jastrow - 1186 - b.h. - פֶּן - pen
 - eventually, lest

'NOT!' 'eventually' means now or ripe.

Spice And Ripe Spicy Plants

A settlement established in the central plains of the Caucasus took the name Tevuz, a place that in modern times produces cotton. Tevuz along with Ganca are two cities that appear to have been in the only flat, sea level rich farmland in the southern Caucasus along the Trade Route.

68

8. Tevuz – City in the nation of Azerbaijan

Jastrow - 1643 - b.h. - תְּבוּאָה - t'vooau
- that which is brought in, grain, provision

Jastrow - 377 - b.h. - ז - zayeen
- formative as a suffix

תְּבוּז - Tevuz

NOT!

Jastrow - 327 - b.h. - הָא - hau
- this, [connotes a daily performance]

A 'NOT' daily performance is a special this.

This Is A Grain Harvest!

With the Caucasus noted for its earthquakes and the city of Yerevan, situated about equidistant between the Caspian Sea and the Black Sea in the Caucasus Mountains at about 15,000 feet, 'earthquake country', the people living in that settlement apparently experienced an earthquake and so named the settlement as a result of an earthquake.

9. Yerevan – City in the nation of Armenia

Jastrow - 596 - b.h. - יְרִיעָה - y'reeau
- to shake

Jastrow - 1454 - b.h. - רוֹב - rov
- multitude, larger portion, majority

Jastrow - 593 - b.h. - יָרֵא - yaurae
- to tremble, fear

Jastrow - 865 - b.h. - נָא - nau
- I pray, prithee

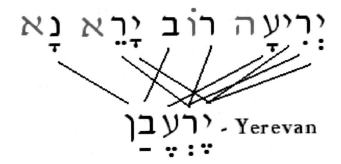

יְרִיעָה רוֹב יָרֵא נָא

יְרֶעֲבֶן - Yerevan

NOT!

Jastrow - 24 - b.h. - אָוָה - to desire, covet

Shaking In Multitudes And Trembling In Fear, We Pray (With) No Desires

----

Mt. Ararat, a mountain in modern day Turkey, is awesome to see from Yerevan, Armenia and was so named 'In Awe Of The Mountain'. It is believed by some to be where Noah's Ark is situated. A large piece of wood found somewhat below a site observed from satellite photos as an anomaly on the snow covered mountain was retrieved by a mountain climbing expedition and was radio carbon dated to be from about 250 B.C.E., more than four hundred years after the Samarian abduction. It is conceivable that the people who lived along the Trade Route in the Caucasus would have prospered tremendously during those previous centuries of trade; and during the summers they would have done what we would do if we were prosperous, take a cool summer vacation and Mt. Ararat was obviously very cool in the summer. With the Caucasus Mountains on a suspected steady rise it is conceivable that a part of Mt. Ararat that is snow covered year round now may well have been merely cool in summer 2,250 years ago. If the mountain rises even two inches a year, in 2,250 years it could rise 4,500 inches or about 375 feet, enough to make a summer cool spot into a summer snow spot. As a summer resort area one would expect several resort hotels to have been built on Mt. Ararat, and since the descendants of the Samarian People most likely still had 'tribal memories' of what was contained in the verbally passed down Torah, with the final redaction of the Torah being in the Fifth Century B.C.E. about three hundred years after the abductions, perhaps using the humor that these people had it is conceivable that the Noah's Ark which people in legend have attributed to have been on top of Mt. Ararat might very well have been on Mt. Ararat, not as Noah's Ark but as a resort hotel in the shape of Noah's Ark. With the upper reaches of Mt. Ararat being a difficult place to get to, one would expect young couples to have found their way up and what better place for young couples to be vacationing two by two in Biblical terms than in Noah's Ark.

10. Mt. Ararat – Mountain in the nation of Turkey

Jastrow - 365 - b.h. - הֶרֶר - herer
- mound, mountain

71

Jastrow - 1502 - רְתֵת = רַתְ - rat = retet

Jastrow - 1504 - b.h. - רְתֵת - retet
- trembling, awe

הָרֵר רַתְ

אֲרָרַת - Ararat

Jastrow - 327 - heh (ה) interchanges with alef (א)

In Awe Of The Mountain

Sumqayit is tucked into a cove formed by the Apseron Peninsula on the west coast of the Caspian Sea due east of Mt. Ararat and appears to have also been a perfect summer vacation place. With Noah's Ark on Mt. Ararat being a resort hotel in the mountains, Sumqayit would have been a seaside community as seaside resorts are today.

11. Sumqayit – City in the nation of Azerbaijan

Jastrow - 1000 - b.h. - סָמַךְ - saumak
- to close, join, to pack, close, stamp

Jastrow - 1358 - p.b.h. - קייטא - kayauytau
- summer, fruits

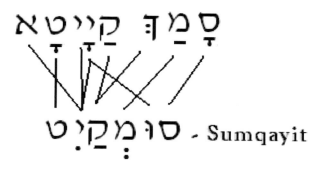

סָמַךְ קייטא

סוּמְקַיִט - Sumqayit

Jastrow - 559 - yod (י) interchanges with alef (א)

Jastrow - 559 - yod (י) interchanges with vav (ו)

To Pack And Join (For The) Summer

As the centuries wore on after the settlement of Vani it became a major source of iron, most likely in shapes of iron bars for blacksmiths to fashion into whatever they would want to make. Tabriz, well south of the Trade Route and rather central to the Middle East, was the place where the iron from Vani would have been sold for distribution throughout the Middle East.

12. Tabriz – City in the nation of Iran

Jastrow - 520 - b.h. - טָחַר - t'khaur
- the pure, real surface (of gold), free from coals or ashes

Jastrow - 191 - b.h. - בַּרְזֶל - barzel
- iron, iron tool

טָחַר בַּרְזֶל

\\\ /

טַבְרֶז - Tabriz

NOT!
Jastrow - 497 - b.h. - חר = חָרַר - khr = khaurar

Jastrow - 506 - b.h. - חָרַר - khaurar
- to glow, to be rough, excited, to burn, to be blackened, charred

Jastrow - 685 - b.h. - ל - lamed
- prefix for unto, to, toward, for

A 'NOT!' lamed at the end of a combined word could mean not a prefix for unto, to, toward or for, but a suffix for unto, to, toward and for.

Pure Iron, Free Of Coals Or Ashes And Not Blackened Or Charred Unto

----

74

As with the Cherkesee who policed the Caucasus west of the Caspian Sea, Kazanka, east of the Caspian Sea, was a place which would have garrisoned Cherkesee types of police, police or guards who would beat up and mutilated thieves, in seclusion, in protecting the merchandise.

13. Kazanka – City in the nation of Kazakhstan

Jastrow - 1396 - b.h. - קָסַם -kausam
-to cut, carve,
(a curse invoking
God as a carver)

Jastrow - 408 - b.h. -זַעַם - zaam
- anger

Jastrow - 1096 - b.h. - עֲנָק - aunauk
- giant

עֲנָק   זַעַם   קָסַם

קָזַנְק - Kazanka

NOT!
Jastrow - 1086 - b.h. - עַם - am
- gathering, crowd,
people

Jastrow - 998 - b.h. - סַם -sam
-drug, medicine, poison

The Giant In Anger Cuts Down Like God Without A Drug Or A Crowd Of People

----

A part of the infrastructure which supported the Trade Route consisted of the transfer of produce from areas like Ganca and Tevuz that grew produce, through the Caucasus to the Caspian Sea, perhaps at Baku, and then shipping them the shortest distance across the Caspian Sea from Baku to a city called Krasnovodsk which was at a recent time called Turkmen Basii after the then leader of the nation of Turkmenistan. The constant flow of produce through Krasnovodsk made it a good place for the authorities to apply a tax and that is what the Samarians or their descendants named or perhaps renamed the settlement, Krasnovodsk, 'Certain To Spring Forth A Tax On The Bags Of Produce Here'.

14. Krasnovodsk – City in the nation of Turkmenistan

Jastrow - 672 - b.h. - כֶּרֶס - keres
- bag, stomach, belly

Jastrow - 883 - b.h. - נוֹב - noov
- growth, bud, to spring forth, flow

Jastrow - 372 - p.b.h. - וַדַּאי - vadaee
- well known, certain, distinct, real

Jastrow - 315 - p.b.h. - דַּסְקָא = טַסְקָא - daskau = taskau

Jastrow - 542 - p.b.h. - טַסְקָא - taskau
- Persian land tax for produce

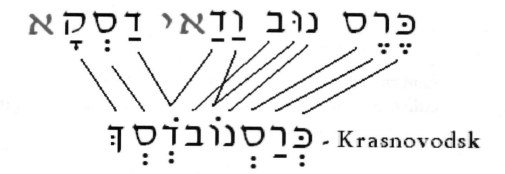

כְּרַס נוּב וַדַאִי דַסְקָא

כְּרַסְנוֹבְדְסְך - Krasnovodsk

NOT!

Jastrow - 559 - p.b.h. - אֵי - yae

" - where?, whither?

A 'NOT!' 'where' is a 'here'.

Certain To Spring Forth A Tax On The Bags Of Produce Here

After the fourth campaign of abduction in 722 B.C.E. and the settlement of the people of the Tribe of Ephraim along the shores of the Caspian Sea, a connection was probably made between Krasnovodsk, the most easterly city on the Caspian Sea, and the original Trade Route, FIGURE II-5, established by the peoples of the tribes of Asher, Naphtali, Zebulun, Manasseh, Gad, and some from Ephraim and Dan, and most likely those from Judah who had settled in the land of the Philistines; all taken during the first and second campaigns, FIGURE I-4. There was probably a great deal of officialdom in making that connection because Nebit Dag appears to have been a military police barracks near the settlement of Nebat, where Nebat was the father of Jeroboam I, the founder of the Northern Kingdom that broke away from the Kingdom of David and Solomon.

15. Nebit Dag – City in the nation of Turkmenistan

Jastrow - 868 - b.h. - נְבָט - Nebat
- The father of Jeroboam I, founder of the Northern Kingdom which broke away from the unified kingdom of David and Solomon in 928 B.C.E.

Jastrow - 280 - b.h. - דֶּגֶל - degel
- troop, division, cohort, standard

נְבָט דֶּגֶל
| | ///
נְבִט־דַג - Nebit Dag

NOT!

Jastrow - 685 - b.h. - ל – lamed
– prefix for: unto, to, toward, for

A 'NOT!' lamed at the end of a combined word could mean not a prefix for unto, to, toward or for but a suffix for unto, to, toward and for.

Nebat – The Military Police Barracks Unto

78

The founding of the settlement of Kazandzhik leading to Gorgan, FIGURE II-5, appears to have also been a seat of government in which the local officials were corrupt without the approval of the central government.

16. Kazandzhik – City in the nation of Turkmenistan

Jastrow - 628 - b.h. - כָּזָב - cauzauv
- falsehood

Jastrow - 81 - p.b.h. - אַנְדִּיסְקֵי - andeeskae
- state officials

כָּזָב אַנְדִּיסְקֵי

קָזָנדְזִיק - Kazandzhik

Jastrow - 947 - The samekh (ס) interchanges with the zayeen (ז)

NOT!

Jastrow - 134 - b.h. - בָּא - bau
- father

Jastrow - 576 - p.b.h. - יי - yee
- oh!, woe!

The Falsehood (Of The) State Officials, Without A Woe, Not The Father

----

It is conceivable that the grain and other produce that grew in Tevuz was transported to Baku, across the Caspian Sea to Krasnovodsk and then on to Nebit Dag and Kazandzhik, the government installations established most likely to protect the produce and the grain which ended up in the settlement of Gorgan where the grain was ground into flour for

79

distribution to the people who settled in the Kara Kum Desert area, in places like Ashkhabad and Kizyl Arvat, FIGURE II-5. Why Gorgan was established to grind flour stems from its location. It lies near the Gorgan River which flows westward from a mountainous region to the Caspian Sea. The terrain provides steep differences in elevation of the river bed which was conducive to the use of water power in the building of water wheel operated flour mills. Apparently the work was hard and some jest appears to have been put into the name showing it 'not suitable for scholars'.

17. Gorgan – City in the nation of Iran

Jastrow - 227 - b.h. - גּוֹרֶן - goren
 - granary, threshing flour, harvesting season

Jastrow - 226 - p.b.h. - גּוּרְגָּנָא - goorgaunau
 - connected with a wheelwork, worked by the pressure of water

גּוֹרֶן גּוּרְגָּנָא

גּוֹרְגַּן - Gorgan

NOT!

Jastrow - 371 - וַו vauv is an abbreviation for אַבָּא

Jastrow - 2 - p.b.h. - אַבָּא - abau
- a title of scholars (less than Rabbi)

The Flour Wheel Worked With The Pressure Of Water (But) Not (By) Scholars

- - - - - - - - - - - - - - - - - -

The caravans probably moved in the desert by night when it was cooler and when they could be navigated by the stars, there being few landmarks in the desert to guide them by day. To guide them toward the settlement in the desert by night, sound was very likely used in the way of young women with high pitched voices making high pitched sounds for the caravans to 'home in on', like a ship's horn or bells sounding in the night. The 'certainly' part emphasizes the advertisement and the word 'summer' refers to the heat and the desert.

18. Kizyl Arvat – City in the nation of Turkmenistan

Jastrow - 1339 - b.h. - קוּץ - koots
- to summer

Jastrow - 579 - b.h. - יְלַל - yaulal
- howl, hollow

Jastrow - 113 - b.h. - אָרַב - aurav
- to lie in wait

Jastrow - 200 - b.h. - בַּת - bat
- servant girl, maiden.

קוּץ יָלַל אָרַב בַּת

קָצִיל אַרְבַת - Kizyl Arvat

NOT!
Jastrow - 371 - p.b.h. - ו - vav
- is it indeed so?

A 'NOT!' 'is it indeed so?' is a 'certainly'.

The Servant Girls Certainly Wait And Howl In The Desert

The name Samarkand describes the preparation of opium and the affect of the opium on people. Modern day Uzbekistan has Samarkand as its capital, and now as well as 2700 years ago lies at the foot of the mountains in which Central Asian opium is grown. The Trade Route apparently not only brought silks and other goods from China, but the Trade Route also transported opium from Central Asia east into China as well as south and west into the Middle East and to the lands that are modern day Turkey and Europe.

82

19. Samarkand – City in the nation of Uzbekistan

Jastrow - 998 - b.h. - סַם - sam
- drug, medicine, poison

Jastrow - 847 - b.h. - מִרְקַחַת - meerkakhat
- druggist's preparation, drug, poison

Jastrow - 1092 - b.h. - עֲנַג - anag
- to feel comfortable

Jastrow - 209 - b.h. - גֵד - gaed
- a rounded off seed grain

סַם מִרְקַחַת עֲנַג גֵד

סַמַרְקַנד - Samarkand

NOT!

Jastrow - 209 - b.h. - גֵג - gaeg
- upper portion, top, apex

Jastrow - 1683 - b.h. - תְעִי - tae
- to move to and fro, to be lost, go astray

Drugs And Druggist's Preparations, (Made From) The Rounded Off Seed Grain Without The Upper Portion, (That Make One) Feel Comfortable Without Being Lost Or Going Astray

Along with legal opium there must have existed those who dealt in illegal opium as there are today; and the illegal opium appeared to have made its way into a settlement that was named Kabul, meaning to receive a stolen measure, most likely of opium, prohibited by law.

20. Kabul – City in the nation of Afghanistan

Jastrow - 1308 - b.h. - קָבַל - kauval
- to seize, to join, meet, correspond, to receive, accept, to take an obligation upon oneself, to contract, agree

Jastrow - 1311 - b.h. - קָבַע - kauva
- to cover, press, overpower, rob

Jastrow - 1307 - b.h. - קַב - kav
- hollow out, arch, measure

Jastrow - 170 - b.h. - בַּל - bal
- not, prohibited from

קָבֹל - Kabul

Jastrow - 1034 - ayeen (ע) interchanges with koof (ק)

To Receive A Stolen Measure Prohibited (By Law)

84

The Pamir Mountain Range has a clearly distinctive appearance with steep peaks and narrow valleys between them making for 'winding pathways'. A large flat plain at its foot was a good place for the caravans to camp, which they did. With the Pamir being almost exactly in the center of the Eurasian continental Trade Route it may have been the most important region of the entire Trade Route. It is therefore conceivable that this would have been the center of the Trade Route where the caravans would meet and according to the definition of Pamir, 'to separate, divide and exchange' goods outside of the 'winding pathways'.

21. Pamir – Mountain range in the nation of Tajikistan

Jastrow - 1182 - b.h. - פָלַל - paulal
  - to separate, divide

Jastrow - 748 - b.h. - מוּר - moor
  - to exchange

פָלַל מוּר

פָמִר - Pamir

NOT!
Jastrow - 698 - b.h. - לוּל - lool
  - winding pathway, passageway, a small room with a staircase leading to the upper rooms.

To Separate, Divide And Exchange Not In The
Winding Pathways

It is also conceivable that the settlement of Khorog, which is near the Pamir Mountains and not far from Samarkand was according to definition a place where scholars met and indulged in intoxicating influences. It was a place near the Pamirs where the various branches of the Trade Route met and where people from all over Eurasia could meet and exchange goods. Khorog being between the Pamir 'trade zone' and the Samarkand source of good opium could be suspected as being a place where ideas and philosophies were exchanged.

22. Khorog – City in the nation of Tajikistan

Jastrow - 436 - b.h. - חוּס - khoos
  - to have affection for

Jastrow - 1435 - b.h. - רָאָה - rauau
  - to meet with

Jastrow - 1448 - b.h. - רָגֶל - raugal
  - to move on, run, a scholar who is an habitual visitor of drinking houses

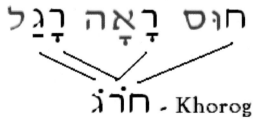

חוּס רָאָה רָגֶל

חוֹרֹג - Khorog

NOT!
Jastrow - 947 - b.h. - סָאָה - sau
  - measure

Jastrow - 371 - ו - vav
  - is it indeed so?

86

Jastrow - 685 - b.h. - ל - lamed

> - prefix for: unto, to, toward, for

A lamed at the end of a combined word could mean not a prefix for unto, to, toward or for but a suffix for unto, to, toward and for.

A 'NOT!' 'is it indeed so?' is a strong 'it is indeed so!'.

It Is Indeed To Meet With And Have Affection For Scholars Who Are Habitual Visitors Of Drinking (Or Smoking) Houses Unto No Measure

----

Ulan Ude is just east of Lake Baykal on a mountain river and with a source of good clay perhaps for pots and other clay items was probably a part of the commercial infrastructure of the Trade Route.

23. Ulan Ude – City in the nation of Russia

Jastrow - 26 - b.h. - אוֹלָם - oolaum

> - in front of, opposite, entrance, hall

Jastrow - 17 - b.h. - אָדַם - audam

> - to be viscous, thick, dark, to be red, grow red

Jastrow - 17 - b.h. - אָדָמַה - adaumau

> - thick and moist, clay

87

אוּלָם אָדָם אֲדָמָה

אוּלָן אוּד - Ulan Ude

NOT!

Jastrow - 794 - מְמַל = מָמָה

Jastrow - 795 - b.h. - מָלַל = מֶמַל

Jastrow - 792 - b.h. - מָלַל - maulal
- to crush

Opposite The Thick Dark Red Clay That Does Not (Need) Crushing

- - - - - - - - - - - - - - - - -

The Hindu Kush region in times prior to settlement by the Samarians was most likely a cultural and religious center for the people of the region; people who were very likely 'beholden to be devoted' to their religion and the region was so named by the Samarian Settlers or more likely their early descendants. Although the Samarian Settlers and their descendants appeared to have respected the Hindus they made it clear that they did not agree with their beliefs.

It is significant to note that the approximately 5000 modern Bnei Menashe People who are Jewish live near the Hindu Kush region in northeastern India and who could have been descended from the original Samarian Settlers, believe that they are descended from the Tribe of Manasseh. Since the Tribe of Manasseh was abducted mostly at the end of the second campaign of abductions they would have been brought into the eastern segment of the Trade Route, right in line with where the Bnei Menashe People are presently located.

24. Hindu Kush – Region in Kashmir, India, Pakistan and Afghanistan

Jastrow - 343 - b.h. - הֵי - hae
- behold, here is

Jastrow - 877 - b.h. - נָדַב - n'dav
- to be devoted to

Jastrow - 441 - b.h. - חוּשׁ - khoosh
- to feel, to feel pain, be affected

הֵי נָדַב חוּשׁ

הֶנְדוּ כּוּשׁ - Hindu Kush

NOT!

Jastrow - 560 - p.b.h. - יָבֵ - yaevau
- it agrees with, corresponds to

To Be Affected (By Those Who Are) Beholden To Be Devoted But Not To Agree With

----

The caravans on the Trade Route obviously needed places at regular intervals to stay and replenish their food and water supplies and Tashkent was apparently one of those rest stops; where a cell could be interpreted in modern English to mean a hotel room.

89

25. Tashkent – City in the nation of Uzbekistan

Jastrow - 1641 - b.h. - תָּא - tau
- cell

Jastrow - 1575 - b.h. - שָׁכַן - shauchan
- to dwell, rest

Jastrow - 132 - b.h. - אֲתָא - atau
- to come, to arrive

תָּא שָׁכַן אֲתָא

תַּשְׁכְנת - Tashkent

Jastrow - 1034 - ayeen (ע) interchanges with alef (א)
NOT!
Jastrow - 99- p.b.h. - אָעָא - auau
- wood, woods

To Arrive And Rest In A Cell Not In The Woods

Wood was obviously a commodity on the Trade Route and Tselinograd, which is somewhat north of the Trade Route in a wooded part of Southern Siberia, was most likely a place where the timber was brought to be cut into lumber for export to other Trade Route locations.

26. Tselinograd (Akmolinsk) – City in the nation of Kazakhstan

Jastrow - 995 - b.h. - סָלַל - saulal
- to make a path, pave, to tread, press

Jastrow - 875 - b.h. - נָגַר - naugar
- to carry along, roll, to scrape, to saw

Jastrow - 275 - b.h. - ד - daled
- of, who, which, that

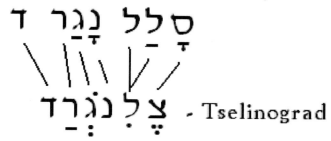

סָלַל נָגַר ד

צֶלָ נָגְרַד - Tselinograd

To Make A Path To Carry Along To Who Scrape and Saw

Tselinograd, a place related to forestry was later named Akmolinsk, a place related to food production. Apparently that very fertile former forest land would have made for very good farming.

27. Akmolinsk (Tselinograd) – City in the nation of Kazakhstan

Jastrow - 63 - b.h. - אֲכִילָה - akheelau
- eating, food, meal, dish

Jastrow - 796 - b.h. - מָן - maun
    - portion, food

Jastrow - 988 - p.b.h. - סַךְ - sak
    - amount, number

אֲכִילָה מָן סַךְ

אַכְּמָלֶנְסְךָ - Akmolinsk

NOT!
Jastrow - 565 - b.h. - יָה - yau
    - Oh! exclamation of distress

There Is No Distress In The Amount Of Food To Eat

Not all of the settlements were apparently always successful and it appears as though a particular city was renamed Novokuzne (tsk), after an apparent loss of a good water supply. As discussed earlier on page 39 under Novosibirsk, the (tsk) (צךְ)could have been put onto Novokuzne at the later time.

28. Novokuznetsk – City in the nation of Russia

Jastrow - 883 - b.h. - נוּב - noov
    - growth, bud, to spring
    forth, flow

92

Jastrow - 883 - b.h. - נוֹב - Nov

- a town in Benjamin

Jastrow - 627-628 - b.h. - כָּזַב - keezav

- to fail, dry up
(of water courses),
to be false, to lie

Jastrow - 406 - b.h. - זָנַח - zaunaukh

- to run to and fro,
wander

Jastrow - 317 - p.b.h. - צַךְ - tsk

- the first letters of the
names of the 2nd and
3rd plagues on Egypt

צַךְ חָנַז כָּזַב נוֹב

(צַךְ) נוֹבכָּזַן - Novokuzne (tsk)

NOT!

Jastrow - 454 - b.h. - חיי - khayee

- to live, to keep alive,
to sustain life

**The Town That Sprang Forth In Growth (Like) Nov Is
Dried Up Cannot Sustain Life (So We) Wander For Water**

Another Trade Route food source was Ubsa Nor, the region which in modern times breeds livestock and camels.

29. Ubsa Nor – City in the nation of Mongolia

Jastrow - 8 - b.h. - אָבַס - auvas
- to fatten, feed

Jastrow - 909 - b.h. - נוֹר - noor
- to break ground, clear [ploughed ground]

אָבַס נוֹר

אוּבֶּס נוֹר - Ubsa-Nor

To Fatten And Feed (Livestock Near) The Ploughed Ground

~~~~~~~~~~~~~~~~~

During the building of Russia's Trans-Siberian Railroad between 1891 and 1916, one of the most difficult places to put railroad tracks was around Lake Baykal because the mountains in that region go directly down into the lake. To place those tracks the builders had to blast away sides of the mountain to cut flat terraces in the cliffs. The region around the city of Irkutsk, which is on the Angara River, seems to have that same problem. In ancient times the Samarian Traders and their descendants who navigated the river had to have used horses to pull the river boats upstream; and it had to have been a very treacherous operation with only narrow flat pathways for footing. The name, Irku (tsk), was most likely derived to describe that difficulty.

30. Irkutsk – City in the nation of Russia

Jastrow - 1123 - b.h. - עָרַץ - auratz
- to be strong, to frighten

Jastrow - 1123 - b.h. - עָרַךְ - aurak
- to pass, to squeeze through, to strap

Jastrow - 1481 - b.h. - רִכְשָׁא - reekhshau
- harnessed horses, war horses

Jastrow - 317 - p.b.h. - צַךְ - tsk
- the first letters of the names of the 2nd and 3rd plagues on Egypt

עָרַץ עָרַךְ רִכְשָׁא צַךְ

(צַךְ) א כ ר עָ - Irku(tsk)

NOT!

Jastrow - 1505 - b.h. - שֵׁץ = שִׁיץ

Jastrow - 1567 - p.b.h. - שִׁיץ - sheetz
- to go forth

(Those Who Are) Frightened To Squeeze Through With
The Horses Will Not Go Forth

95

Going through the deserts and mountains of Mongolia was difficult work and the men who drove the caravans had to have had a great need to relax; so places like Ulan Batur, Sukhe Bator and Sukh Batar were established. The term 'not be bent or tired' could mean to have had a massage and/or some puffs of opium.

31. Ulan Batur – City in the nation of Mongolia

Jastrow - 26 - b.h. - אוּלָם - oolaum
- in front of, opposite

Jastrow - 699 - b.h. - לוּן - loon
- stay overnight

Jastrow - 200 - b.h. - בַּת - bat
- daughter, maiden, girl, servant girl

Jastrow - 200 - b.h. - בַּת - bat
- bath, a measure

Jastrow - 526 - b.h. - טוּר - toor
- mountain

Jastrow - 201 - b.h. - בֶּתֶר - beter
- to cut, piece, decree, allotment [fee]

Jastrow - 200 - b.h. - בְּתוּלָה - btoolau
- untouched, virgin

Jastrow - 1694 - b.h. - תּ׳רעה - t'rah
- bad manners, depravity, degenerate child

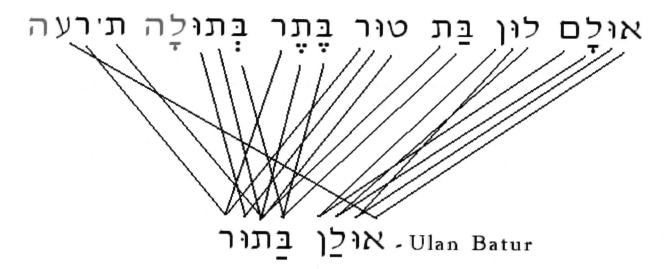

אוּלָן בַּתוּר - Ulan Batur

NOT!

Jastrow - 693 - p.b.h. - לְהִי - lhee
- to be bent, tired

To Stay Overnight In Front Of The Mountain (For A) Fee, (Have A) Bath, Not Be Bent Or Tired (And Show) Bad Manners (With) An Untouched Virgin Girl

----

32. Sukhe Bator – City in the nation of Russia

Jastrow - 962 - b.h. - סוֹחֵר - sookhaer
- traveler, beggar

Jastrow - 962 - b.h. - סוּחַ - sooakh
- to think, to talk, to tell

Jastrow - 962 - b.h. - סוּחָא - sookhau
- that which is thrown out, dirt, disgusting matter [be washed]

Jastrow - 963 - b.h. - סוּךְ - sook
- to pour oil, to oil

Jastrow - 200 - b.h. - בַּת - bat
- bath, a measure

Jastrow - 200 - b.h. - בַּת - bat
- daughter, maiden, girl, servant girl

Jastrow - 201 - b.h. - בֶּתֶר - beter
- to cut, piece, decree, allotment [fee]

Jastrow - 200 - b.h. - בְּתוּלָה - btoolau
- untouched, virgin

Jastrow - 526 - b.h. - טוּר - toor
- mount, mountain

Jastrow - 1694 - b.h. - תּ'רעה - t'rah
- bad manners, depravity, degenerate child

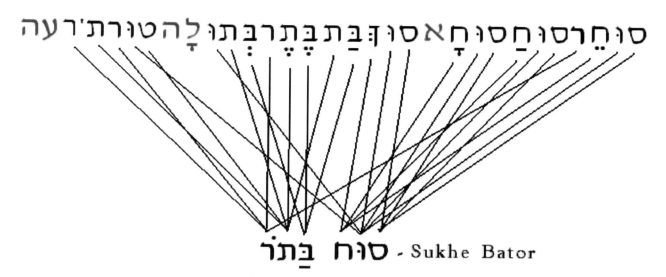

סוּחֶרְסוּחֲסוּחָאסוּזְבַּתבֶּתֶּרְבָּתוּלָהטוּרַת'רְעֹה

סוּח בַּתֹר - Sukhe Bator

Jastrow - 1034 - ayeen (ע) interchanges with alef (א)

NOT!

Jastrow - 66 - b.h. - אַלָה - alau
- pointed, prominent

(Near) The Mountain A Traveler, (For A) Fee, Can Be
Washed In A Bath, Have Oils Poured On Him, (Show) Bad
Manners With An Untouched Virgin Girl And Not (Be)
Pointed (At) And Talk And Tell (Of His Travels)

99

33. Sukh Batar – Region in the nation of Mongolia

Jastrow - 962 - b.h. - סוֹחֵר - sookhaer
- traveler, beggar

Jastrow - 962 - b.h. - סוּחַ - sooakh
- to think, to talk, to tell

Jastrow - 962 - b.h. - סוּחָא - sookhau
- that which is thrown out, dirt, disgusting matter [be washed]

Jastrow - 963 - b.h. - סוּךְ - sook
- to pour oil, to oil

Jastrow - 200 - b.h. - בַּת - bat
- bath, a measure

Jastrow - 200 - b.h. - בַּת - bat
- daughter, maiden, girl, servant girl

Jastrow - 201 - b.h. - בֶּתֶר - beter
- to cut, piece, decree, allotment [fee]

Jastrow - 200 - b.h. - בְּתוּלָה - btoolau
- untouched, virgin

Jastrow - 526 - b.h. - טוּר - toor
- mount, mountain

Jastrow - 1694 - b.h. - תִּרְעָה - t'rah
- bad manners, depravity, degenerate child

100

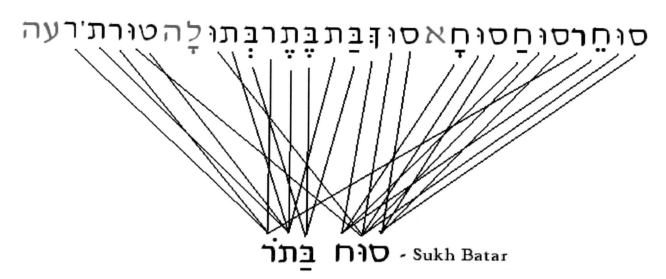

סוֹחֵ בַּתֹּר - Sukh Batar

Jastrow - 1034 - ayeen (ע) interchanges with alef (א)

NOT!
Jastrow - 66 - b.h. - אַלָה - alau
- pointed, prominent

(Near) The Mountain A Traveler, (For A) Fee, Can Be
Washed In A Bath, Have Oils Poured On Him, (Show)
Bad Manners With An Untouched Virgin Girl And Not
(Be) Pointed (At) And Talk And Tell (Of His Travels)

101

Another product along the Trade Route would have been salt which, in the form of sodium, is a product of Uniket in modern times.

34. Uniket – City in the nation of China

Jastrow - 339 - b.h. - הוֹן - hon
- possession, wealth

Jastrow - 512 - b.h. - חָתָה - khautau
- to dig, to take coals out with a pan

הוֹן חָתָה
\ \ //
וּנִכֵּת - Uniket

NOT!
Jastrow - 335 - b.h. - הָה - hauh
- ah alas!, be grieving for

To Possess Wealth By Digging Without Grief

Another probable resting place for caravans in the mountainous desert of southern Mongolia was Khana Abasa.

35. Khana Abasa – City in the nation of China

Jastrow - 482 - b.h. - חָנָה - khaunau
- to encamp

Jastrow - 8 - b.h. - אָבַס - auvas
- to stuff, fatten, feed

אָבַס   חָנָה

אַבַּס   חָנָה - Khana Abasa

To Encamp And Feed

In places where there would have been indigenous peoples, the situation was a lot more risky than in the mostly uninhabited desert and mountains where most of the Trade Route existed. Modern day Kirin stands in a forested region which also grows cereals; so in ancient times there may very well have been indigenous peoples living near Kirin. If the Samarian Settlers were to have provided a rest stop for the caravans they would certainly had to have protected them, and that is what they apparently did in the building of the fortified city of Kirin.

36. Kirin – City in the nation of China

Jastrow - 1368 - b.h. - קִיר - keer
                  - surrounding enclosure,
                     wall, recess, chamber

Jastrow - 1095 - b.h. - עָנָן - aunaun
                  - cover, protection

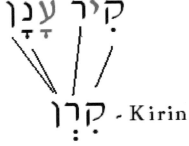

קָרֶן - Kirin

NOT!
Jastrow - 583 - p.b.h. - יַעָא - y'au
                  - to burst forth, bloom

A Surrounding Enclosure (For) Protection Not To Burst Forth (Merchandise)

Like Khana Abasa, Lupeh was probably a rest stop but also a trading place for caravans but unlike Khana Abasa, Lupeh was in the desert where the caravans must have traveled at night when it was cool with the caravan drivers guiding themselves by the stars. In that situation they would have needed 'something' to 'home in on' to find the settlement. In Kizyl Arvat in the Kara Kum Desert (page 81 of this text) there were 'servant girls who howled in the night' for the caravan drivers to 'home in on', and in Lupeh there were torches not fired by wood.

37. Lupeh – City in the nation of China

Jastrow - 699 - b.h. - לוּן - loon
- to stay overnight

Jastrow - 715 - b.h. - לַפִּיד - lapeed
- torch

Jastrow - 1137 - b.h. - פָדַע - pauda
- to redeem

Jastrow - 1130 - b.h. - פָּאֵה - paeau
- to split, divide

לוּן לַפִּיד פָּדַע פָּאֵה

לוּפֶה - Lupeh

Jastrow - 559 - yod(י) interchanges with alef(א)
NOT!

Jastrow - 877 - b.h. - נָדַד - needad
- to make unsteady

Jastrow - 99 - p.b.h. - אָעַ - au
- wood, woods

The Steady Torch Without Wood (In The Desert) To Stay Overnight And Redeem And Divide

----

With Lupeh being in the desert the question arises as to where the inhabitants got the fuel for the torches. In the region around modern day Beijing, somewhat near modern day Ulanhot, there are modern day coal fields. In the definition of Ulanhot caravans can be seen ready to approach those coal fields. In finding the Hebrew root for the word fragment 'hot' in Ulanhot, liberties were taken in extrapolating the pronunciation for 'hot' to 'khot' which gives the coal definition to the city names of Ulanhot, Silinhot, Huhehot and Bayinhot.

38. Ulanhot – City in the nation of China

Jastrow - 26 - b.h. - אוּלָם - oolaum
- front of, opposite, entrance hall

Jastrow - 512 - b.h. - חָתָה - khautau
- to dig, especially to take coals out with a pan

אוּלָם חָתָה

אוּלַנְהֹת - Ulanhot

Jastrow - 415 - The khet (ח) interchanges with the heh (ה)

Entrance (To Where) The Coals Are Dug

On the way to the mountainous coal fields from the desert Trade Route a rest stop for the caravans' drivers was apparently Silinhot.

39. Silinhot – City in the nation of China

Jastrow - 964 - b.h. - סוּלָם - soolaum
- ascent, ladder

Jastrow - 995 - b.h. - סָלַל - saulal
- to tread, to pass, to make a path

Jastrow - 512 - b.h. - חָתָה - khautau
- to dig, especially to take coals out with a pan

סָלְנִהֹת - Silinhot

Jastrow - 791 - a mem (מ,ם) interchanges with a noon (נ)

NOT!

Jastrow - 371 - וֹ - vav
- is it indeed so?

A 'NOT!' 'is it indeed so?' is an 'it is indeed so!'.

To Ascend In A Path Indeed To The Coals

At Huhehot the caravans reached the coal fields.

40. Huhehot – City in the nation of China

Jastrow - 338 - b.h. - הָוָה - hauvau
                 - to exist, to be, become,
                     to occur, come to pass

Jastrow - 512 - b.h. - הָתָה - hautau
                - to dig, especially to take
               coals out with a pan

הָוָה הָתָה

הוּהֵהֹת - Huhehot

To Be (In The) Digging Of Coals

West of Huhehot the Samarians and/or their descendants were apparently prospecting for more coal from their settlement of Bayinhot with the apparent caution to 'not get too excited'.

41. Bayinhot – City in the nation of China

Jastrow - 181 - b.h. - בְּעִי - b'ae
- to search, inquire, ask

Jastrow - 581 - b.h. - יָנַן - yaunan
- to move quickly, to glisten, be bright

Jastrow - 512 - b.h. - הָתָה - hautau
- to dig, especially to take coals with a pan

בְּעִי יָנַן הָתָה

בִּינהֹת - Bayinhot

NOT!

Jastrow - p.b.h. - יְעָא - y'au
- to burst forth, bloom

To Move Quickly And Brightly In Search Of The Coal But Not To Burst Forth

----

New peoples and nations resulting from interactions between the Samarians and their descendants and the Scythians and other indigenous peoples of their adopted lands appear to have kept the Hebrew language as their base language. The word part 'stan' in the names of many nations appears to have come from the Hebrew word 's'taun', meaning hostile being or disturber which can be interpreted as meaning new people coming in to disturb the status quo. The Samarians and their descendants appear to have always looked at themselves as those new people and so they called themselves the new people and their nations, the nations of the new people, the 'Stan' countries. Again, the orange colored definitions are of nations and cities shown in FIGURE II-5 and the burgundy colored definitions are of peoples and nations not in FIGURE II-5.

FIGURE II-4-A

LIST OF DEFINED IN ENGLISH NAMES OF PEOPLES AND NATIONS GIVEN AFTER THE ESTABLISHMENT OF THE TRADE ROUTE

1. Kazakhstan – The nation of Kazakhstan
– 'New People To Trim The Thorns'

2. Turkmenistan – The nation of Turkmenistan
– 'These Are The New People Who Toil And Labor For Food'

3. Hayastan – The nation of Armenia
– 'Behold The New People'

4. Afghanistan – The nation of Afghanistan
– 'Also In This Paradise (There Are) New People'

5. Pashtoon – A people in Afghanistan
– 'Split Off In Willful Rebellion To Straighten (Our) Integrity (Or) Not To Live'

6. Kandahar – City in the nation of Afghanistan
       – 'To Dig A Base Of Reason'

7. Kyrgyzstan – The nation of Kyrgyzstan
       – 'The New People Who Lay Out A Path With Markers Before (They Collect) A Tax'

8. Kyrgyzstan – The nation of Kyrgyzstan
       – 'The New People In A Surrounding Enclosure Of Hewn Stone, Not To Be Hanged For Robbery'

9. Baykal – Region and lake in the nation of Russia
       – 'To Provide For All Households That Live In The District But Not To Engrave'

10. Buryat – City in the nation of Russia
       – 'A Covenant To Have No Rule Here And (To Use) The Tools To Clear The Forest (Near) The Lake For A Surplus'

11. Ashgabat – City in the nation of Turkmenistan
       – 'Daughter Of Wisdom'

12. Tajikistan – The nation of Tajikistan
       – 'The New People (Who) Command The Northern Gate'

13. Uzbekistan – The nation of Uzbekistan
       – 'The New People Of The Entrance Into The Finger Not The Woods'

FIGURE II-4-B

DEVELOPMENT OF ENGLISH DEFINITIONS OF NAMES OF PEOPLES AND NATIONS GIVEN AFTER THE ESTABLISHMENT OF THE TRADE ROUTE

Kazakhstan, situated mostly in uninhabited hill and desert regions was a place for nomadic herding and was called the nation of 'New People To Trim The Thorns'; where 'to trim the thorns' is most likely to herd animals who feed on the thorny brush in the desert.

1. Kazakhstan – The nation of Kazakhstan

Jastrow - 652 - b.h. - כָּסַח - kausakh
- to cut down, trim, clear of thorns

Jastrow - 1554 - b.h. - שָׂטָן - s'taun
- hostile being, disturber, accuser, [new people]

כָּסַח שָׂטָן

כָּזַחְשְׁטָן - Kazakhstan

Jastrow - 947 - The samekh (ס) interchanges with the zayeen (ז)

New People To Trim The Thorns

Much of Turkmenistan is desert and it was apparently very difficult to grow food; and still calling themselves the new people, the Turkmenistanis named themselves 'The New People Who Toil And Labor For Food'.

2. Turkmenistan – The nation of Turkmenistan

Jastrow - 526 - b.h. - טוֹרַח - torakh
- toil, labor, trouble, painstaking preparations

Jastrow - 796 - b.h. - מָנָה - maunau
- portion, food

Jastrow - 1554 - b.h. - שָׂטֵן - s'taun
- hostile being, disturber, accuser [new people]

טוֹרַח מָנָה שָׂטֵן

טוּרְקְמֶנִשְׂטֵן - Turkmenistan

NOT!
Jastrow - 327 - הֵ - heh
- is it not?

A 'NOT!' 'is it not?' is a definate is!'.

These Are The New People Who Toil And Labor For Food

The name Hae, meaning 'behold, here is' is the name that the Armenian People reportedly prefer to use in reference to themselves and the 'stan' portion of the name Hayastan refers to the people as the 'new people'. Resultantly, the name Hayastan is the name that the people of Armenia reportedly would prefer their country to be referred to as instead of Armenia.

3. Hayastan (Armenia)

Jastrow - 343 - b.h. - הֵי - hae
        - behold, here is

Jastrow - 1554 - b.h. - שָׂטָן - staun
        - hostile being, disturber, accuser [new people]

הֵי שָׂטָן

הַיְשָׂטָן - Hayastan

Behold The New People

Afghanistan was a good place to live, a paradise, a place to grow things perhaps referring to opium; a place also settled by 'new people' where perhaps earlier people also lived.

4. Afghanistan – The nation of Afghanistan

Jastrow - 99 - b.h. - אַף - af
        - also, too, the same

Jastrow - 256 - b.h. - גַּן - gan
- fenced in place, garden, paradise, place of future reward

Jastrow - 1554 - b.h. - שָׂטֵן - s'taun
- hostile being, disturber, accuser, [new people]

אַף גַּן שָׂטֵן

\\\ |\//

אַפְגָנְשָׂטֵן - Afghanistan

Also In This Paradise (There Are) New People

With Kabul, the modern capital of Afghanistan being the 'place that received stolen measures', most likely of opium prohibited by law, certain people apparently refrained from that enterprise and escaped from it southward splitting off from the Trade Route to 'straighten their integrity'. These were the Pashtoon People.

5. Pashtoon– A people in Afghanistan

Jastrow - 1245 - b.h. - פָּשַׁח - paushakh
- to split, to tear

Jastrow - 1247 - b.h. - פָּשַׁע - pausha
- to be willful,
rebellious,
to pass beyond

Jastrow - 1245 - b.h. - פָּשַׁט - paushat
- to stretch, to
straighten

Jastrow - 1653 - b.h. - תֹּם - tom
- simplicity, integrity

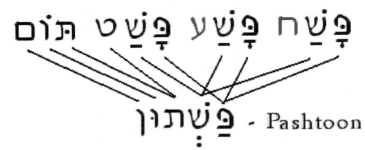

פָּשַׁח פָּשַׁע פָּשַׁט תֹּם

פַּשְׁתּוּן - Pashtoon

Jastrow - 1034 - alef (א) interchanges with ayeen (ע)

Jastrow - 415 - חָאִי (khauee) is the participle of
חַיִי (khayee)

NOT!
Jastrow - 454 - b.h. - חַיי - khayee
- to live

**Split Off In Willful Rebellion To Straighten (Our) Integrity
(Or) Not To Live**

The city of Kandahar was apparently founded by the Pashtoon People to be 'a base of reason' for them away from the drug traffic and to this day the greatest percentage of Pashtoon People living in any one place appear to be living in Kandahar.

6. Kandahar – City in the nation of Afghanistan

Jastrow - 647 - b.h. - כֵּן - kaen
- base, stand, rest

Jastrow - 316 - b.h. - דֵעָה - daeau
- knowledge, understanding, reason, view, taste

Jastrow - 320 - b.h. - דָקַר - daukar
- to dig, bore, pierce

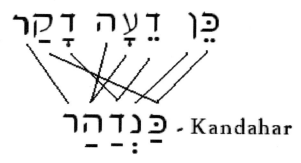

כֵּן דֵעָה דָקַר

כַּנְדְהַר - Kandahar

Jastrow - 1034 - ayeen (ע) interchanges with heh (ה)

To Dig A Base Of Reason

Kyrgyzstan is located in the Alay Mountain Range containing the only pass through the mountains between Tashkent and China. A logical place for a 'turnpike'.

117

7. Kyrgyzstan – The nation of Kyrgyzstan

Jastrow - 664 - p.b.h. - כַּרְגָּא - kargau
- capitation tax, tax, tribute

Jastrow - 263 - p.b.h. - גֵּץ - gaetz
- white earth, chalk, a cross-path laid out with whitened pegs of baked mud or clay

Jastrow - 1554 - b.h. - שָׂטָן - s'taun
- hostile being, disturber, accuser, [new people]

כַּרְגָּא גֵּץ שָׂטָן

כרגז שַׂטָן - Kyrgyzstan

Jastrow -1256- tsadee (צ, ץ) interchanges with zayeen (ז)

NOT!

Jastrow - 1 - א - alef
- upon, over (as a prefix)

A 'NOT!' upon is a 'before'.

The New People Who Lay Out A Path With Markers Before (They Collect) A Tax

----

Taking another route to the definition of the Kyrgyz part of Kyrgyzstan ends in the definition of a place where it seems that the Samarians or their descendants built a prison to keep from having to hang robbers. So, they provided a safe turnpike and a place to put robbers.

8. Kyrgyzstan – The nation of Kyrgyzstan

Jastrow - 1368 - b.h. - קִיר - keer
  -surrounding enclosure, wall, recess, chamber

Jastrow - 230 - b.h. - גָּזִית - gauzeet
  - hewn stone, wall of squared stones

Jastrow - 230 - b.h. - גָּזַל - gauzal
  - to take illegitimately, to tear away, rob

Jastrow - 1554 - b.h. - שָׂטָן - s'taun
  - hostile being, disturber, accuser, [new people]

קִיר גָּזִית גָּזַל שָׂטָן

קִרְגִזְשַׂטָן - Kyrgyzstan

NOT!

Jastrow - 1671 - b.h. - תְּלִי - t'laee
  -to lift up, to suspend, hang, [to be hanged]

The New People In A Surrounding Enclosure Of Hewn Stone, Not To Be Hanged For Robbery

119

Baykal, another place of escape from the Trade Route is in a forested wilderness along the western shore of Lake Baykal well north of the Trade Route. It appears to have been settled well after the establishment of the Trade Route much for the same reasons that the early American Colonists escaped British rule and went into the forested wilderness of North America where there were no wars, taxes or governments in order to take care of their families, themselves, and their neighbors – with no government. The term engrave in the Hebrew 'word analysis' definition should be interpreted as meaning to list.

9. Baykal – Mountain region and lake in the nation of Russia

Jastrow - 167 - b.h. - בַּיִת - bayeet
- house, household, home

Jastrow - 643 - b.h. - כִּלְכֵּל - keelkael
- to surround, to sustain, to provide with everything

Jastrow - 638 - b.h. - כֹּל - kol
- all, every one

Jastrow - 638 - b.h. - כִּכָּר - keekaur
- district

Jastrow - 454 - b.h. - חַיי - khai
- to live

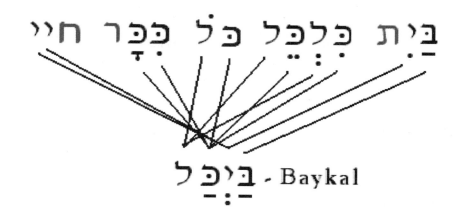

בֵּית כִּלְכֵּל כָּל כִּכֵּר חֵיי

בַּיכֵּל - Baykal

NOT!

Jastrow - 507 - b.h. - חָרַת - khaurat

- to engrave

To Provide For All Households That Live In The District But Not To Engrave

----

Buryat like Baykal appeared to have been established as a place to escape from the Trade Route; and like the Baykal Mountain Region it adjoins Lake Baykal but is east of the lake and north of the Trade Route in a forested mountain wilderness. It has a defined name similar to that of Baykal but with more detail with respect to clearing land and farming.

10. Buryat – Region in the nation of Russia

Jastrow - 194 - b.h. - בְּרִית - breet
                - circle, ring, chain, oath
                  of fidelity, solemn
                  injunction, treatise,
                  covenant

Jastrow - 603 - b.h. - יָתֵד - yautaed
                - something fastened,
                  driven in, peg, nail, handle
                  of a tool

Jastrow - 188 - b.h. - בַּר - bar
                - empty, open, uncultivated
                  ground, forest, prairie

Jastrow - 189 - b.h. - בַּר - bar
                - clear, bright, clean, pure

Jastrow - 194 - b.h. - בְּרֵכָה - braechau
                - pond, lake

Jastrow - 605 - b.h. - יִתְרוֹן - yeetron
                - surplus, difference

בְּרִית - Buryat

NOT!

Jastrow - 300 - b.h. - דון - doon
        - to rule, to hold court, pass
         sentence, punish

Jastrow - 614 - b.h. - כֹּה - coh
        - here, thus

A Covenant To Have No Rule Here And (To Use) The Tools To Clear The Forest (Near) The Lake For A Surplus

----

Ashkhabad appears to have been named as one of the earliest settlements in the 734 to 722 B.C.E. time frame, whereas Ashgabat was renamed most likely in the Twentieth Century C.E. What is very important about this name change is that Ashkhabad which means a settlement requiring strong men to live in was renamed, with just a few changes in consonants, Ashgabat which has a very opposite meaning, the 'daughter of wisdom', which is a smart woman. So, in the Twentieth Century C.E. apparently people who speak modern Turkic recognized a word meaning 'with large testicles alone', a strong man, and humorously with the few consonantal changes turned it into a name meaning a smart woman, the 'Daughter (Of) Wisdom'. From the Biblical Hebrew to the modern Turkic the meanings appear to be the same showing that the languages are basically the same. This acts as a 'peg' which further supports the results of this study showing that the Samarians were brought north to establish the east-west Trade Route through Central Asia.

11. Ashgabat – City in the nation of Turkmenistan – (the same city as Ashkhabad)

Jastrow - 369 - b.h. - הַשְׂכֵּל - haskael
- reflection, wisdom

Jastrow - 200 - b.h. - בַּת - bat
- daughter, maiden, girl, servant girl

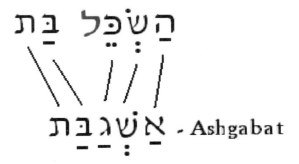

אַשְׁגַבַת - Ashgabat

Jastrow - 327 - heh (ה) interchanges with alef (א)

Jastrow - 201 - geemel (ג) interchanges with kaf (כ)

Since the name Ashgabat was probably coined very recently, within the past hundred years, the 'NOT!' rule would probably not hold, so the lamed (ל) is dropped.

Daughter (Of) Wisdom

The Pamir 'trading center', which is in modern day Tajikistan, being near the northwestern China – India border on the Trade Route, could have been considered as a most important northern trading place in the post Babylonian Exile Period; and so the region around the Pamirs was given the name, 'The Northern Gate', (from India and China)and the inhabitants of the 'The Northern Gate','The New People (Who) Command The Northern Gate'. This Babylonian Exile Period naming is evidenced by the post Biblical Hebrew root word taudee (ׂטדי) which had to have come to the Trade Route after the 597 and 586 B.C.E. exile periods.

The two consonantal spellings of Tadzhikistan and Tajikistan were found on two different maps and no meaningful definitions could be found using the 'zhik' root; but combining the two spellings, Tadzhik and Tajik and leaving out the 'zh' in forming the name Tadjik results in the following definition.

12. Tajikistan – The nation of Tajikistan

Jastrow - 520 - p.b.h. - ׂטדי - taudee
- name of a northern gate of the Temple

Jastrow - 304 - דׂיק = דוק - deek = dook

Jastrow - 287 - דוק = דוך - dook = dook

Jastrow - 285 - p.b.h. - דוך - dook
- to muster, marked off, pointed out, place, stand, hall; leader, chief, commander

125

Jastrow - 1554 - b.h. - שָׂטָן - s'taun
- hostile being, disturber, accuser, [new people]

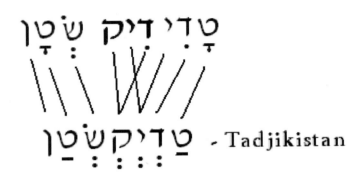

טָדִי דִיק שָׂטָן

טַדִיקשָׂטָן - Tadjikistan

The New People (Who) Command The Northern Gate

Uzbekistan runs north to south from the Aral Sea along what appears to be a mountain divide and reaches Samarkand in the most southern part of Uzbekistan just west of a wooded area. So, the Hebrew 'word analysis' definition of Uzbek, 'Enter Into The Finger Not The Woods', could have been derived from the finger shaped path leading from the Aral Sea with instructions to Samarkand's customers to bear away from the woods and by so doing reach Samarkand, the place where opium was sold.

126

13. Uzbekistan – The nation of Uzbekistan

Jastrow - 110 - b.h. - אֶצְבַּע - etzbah
- finger, index finger

Jastrow - 185 - b.h. - בָּקָא - bakau
- to enter into, search

Jastrow - 1554 - b.h. - שָׂטָן - s'taun
- hostile being, disturber accuser, [new people]

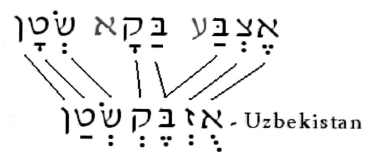

אֶצְבַּע בָּקָא שָׂטָן

אֻזְבֶּקִשְׂטָן - Uzbekistan

Jastrow - 1256 - tsadee (צ) interchanges with zayeen (ז)

NOT!

Jastrow - 99 - p.b.h. - אָץ - auh
- wood, woods

The New People Of The Entrance Into The Finger Not The Woods

FIGURE II-5 maps out the Trade Route established by the abducted Samarian settlers and their descendants as found through this study. The dark blue colored names of countries, cities and places represent the original settlements' and places' names, and the orange colored names of countries, cities and places show the names given to the settlements and places after the establishment of the Trade Route and represent the development of commercial specialites performed in those towns and places, like advertisements.

Mosul – Modern day cities, countries and places named by the Samarian Settlers, in dark blue

Khorog – Modern day cities and countries named after the establishment of the Trade Route by Samarian Settlers or their descendants, in orange

CHINA – Names of modern day cities, countries and landmarks, in black

Volga – Names of modern day rivers, in light blue

— Boundary of the Kingdom of Samaria in 734 B.C.E.

PLACEMENT OF HEBREW 'WORD ANALYSIS' LOCATIONS
FIGURE II-5

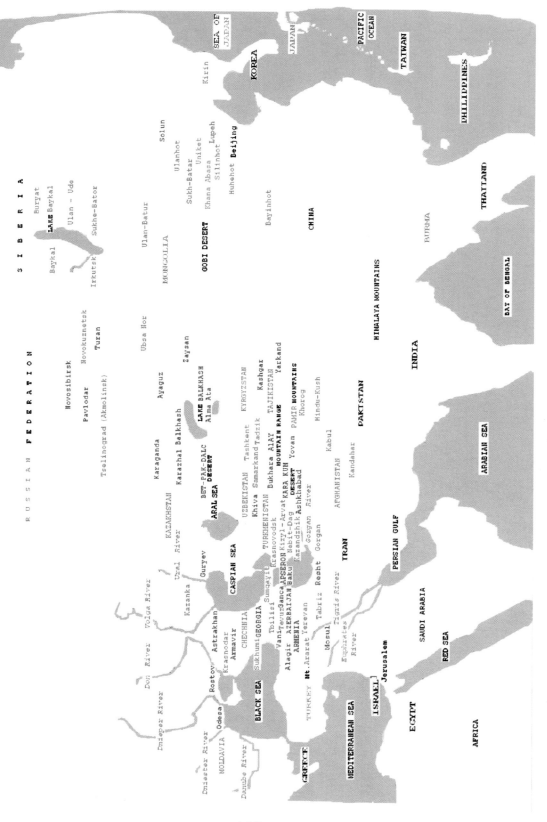

129

FIGURE II-5 completes the part of this study describing where the Ten Lost Tribes of Israel went. The remainder of the study will show some of their legacies. It will show who some of their descendants were along with some of the affects of their existence on our modern world.

SECTION III – DESCENDANTS OF THE LOST TRIBES

There was nothing to keep the Samarians and their descendants from going up the rivers of Europe: the Dnieper, the Danube, the Volga, the Don and the others to trade and to mingle with the inhabitants and to develop into peoples displaying the intelligence of the Samarians and the tactics and behaviors of the indigenous peoples including the Scythians to eventually form peoples such as the the Rus and the Prus and then the Barbarians: the Huns, Vandals, Angles, Saxons, Vikings and others. The same was true in the east where the Mongols appeared to have developed from the Samarian Settlers and their descendants and the indigenous peoples found there.

Where the Samarians and their descendants came upon indigenous peoples whom they did not integrate with they appeared to have named them as they named themselves, according to the languages of the Samarians and their descendants which were based on ancient Hebrew.

The defined transliterations of the names of the Samarian Descendant and indigenous peoples whom they named reflect what the Samarian Descendants did and felt about themselves and what they felt about those other peoples.

Among the names that they gave themselves were the Rus, 'The People Who Run the Course With The Burden On Their Shoulders', who apparently became the merchants of the north going between Scandinavia, Northern Germany, Northern Poland and Russia, up and down through the rivers establishing settlements and becoming the dominant cultures wherever they went.

In places where the Samarian Traders and their descendants didn't intermarry with the native peoples, they left their languages as the dominant languages of those peoples.

These strong, tough, smart people probably traded all through Europe and Asia during the millennium between 734 B.C.E. and the Third Century C.E. when their probable descendants, the Barbarians, came rushing out of their native lands.

Among the Barbarian Descendants of the Samarians were the Huns who came west from the steppes of Central Asia in the Fourth and Fifth Centuries C.E., the Vandals who came out of modern day Eastern Germany in the Fifth Century C.E. to attack the Romans, the Angles and the Saxons who came out of modern day Northern Germany and into Britain in the Fifth and Sixth Centuries C.E. for conquest and resettlement and the Vikings who according to history traded and then pillaged and explored during a two hundred year period from around 790 C.E. to 1066 C.E. In the east the Mongols under Genghis Khan came out of eastern Asia, modern day Mongolia, from about 1200 C.E. until the death of Genghis Khan in 1227 C.E. Then the kingdom fractured with small remnants remaining until 1502 C.E.

A people who appeared to have not been descendants of the Samarian Traders but who adopted their language were the Cossacks who appeared in the Fifteenth Century C.E. while the Mongol empires were disintegrating.

Eventually the Barbarians developed into modern peoples like the Turks, and all of the 'Stan' peoples as well as Russians, Germans, English, Mongolians and Japanese.

Some of the names of peoples and places were formed by Samarian Descendants and some by post 597 B.C.E. Judean and then Jewish merchants who although using the everyday vernacular of their conquering or host countries and cultures, used religious Hebrew regularly in religious matters, and perhaps in certain social and business matters too. The names of the Norman, British and Norse peoples and the lands of Sicily, Denmark, and Burma could have fit into that latter category.

FIGURE III-1-A

LIST OF DEFINED IN ENGLISH NAMES OF FIRST SAMARIAN MILLENNIUM, 8TH CENTURY B.C.E. - 3RD CENTURY C.E., DESCENDANTS OF THE SAMARIANS

1. Rus – '(The People Who) Run The Course With The Burden On Their Shoulders'

2. Russian – 'He Who Is A Rus And Who Helps The Customer To Load Without A Care So As To Bend His Animosity'

3. Prussian – 'He Who Splits The Rus'

FIGURE III-1-B

DEVELOPMENT OF ENGLISH DEFINITIONS OF NAMES OF FIRST SAMARIAN MILLENNIUM, 8TH CENTURY B.C.E. - 3RD CENTURY C.E., DESCENDANTS OF THE SAMARIANS

1. Rus

Jastrow - 1463 - b.h. - רוץ - rootz
- to run (with the burden on his shoulders)

Jastrow - 1475 - p.b.h. - ריס - rees
- course

רוּצָ רִיס

רוּס - Rus

Jastrow - 1256 - tsadee (צ,ץ) interchanges with samekh (ס)

Jastrow - 559 - yod (י) interchanges with vav (ו)

(The People Who) Run The Course With The Burden On
Their Shoulders

The good merchant always helps the customer as did the Russians.

2. Russian

Jastrow - 1463 - b.h. - רוּץ - rootz
 - to run (with the burden
 on his shoulders)

Jastrow - 1475 - p.b.h. - רִיס - rees
 - course

Jastrow - 52 - p.b.h. - אֵינָא - eenau
 - he who

Jastrow - 1537 - b.h. - שׂוֹנֵא - shonae
 - hater, enemy, [to
 help the enemy to
 load so as to bend
 his animosity], [the
 customer]

134

רוֹסְסָאן - Russian

Jastrow - 1256 - tsadee (צ,ץ) interchanges with samekh (ס)

Jastrow - 1505 - sheen (שׁ) interchanges with samekh (ס)

NOT!

Jastrow - 576 - b.h. - יי - yauy
- oh! woe!

He Who Is A Rus And Who Helps The Customer To Load Without A Care So As To Bend His Animosity

----

Between modern day Scandinavia and Russia which were the lands of the Rus there were the Prus, or the Prussians. The people who split the Rus.

3. Prussian

Jastrow - 1130 - b.h. - פֵּי - pae
- to split, divide

135

רוּס - Rus

Jastrow - 52 - p.b.h. - אִינָא - eenau
- he who

פֵּירוּס אִינָא

פְּרוּשַׁאַן - Prussian

Jastrow - 559 - yod (י) interchanges with vav (ו)

He Who Splits The Rus

FIGURE III-2-A

LIST OF DEFINED IN ENGLISH NAMES OF INDIGENOUS PEOPLES AND PLACES FOUND BY SAMARIANS AND THEIR DESCENDANTS AND BY POST 597 B.C.E. JUDEAN AND JEWISH MERCHANTS DURING THE FIRST SAMARIAN MLLENNIUM, 8TH CENTURY B.C.E.-3RD CENTURY C.E.

1. **Teuton** – '(Those Who Are) Loaded With Charms And Ornaments For Frontlets But Who Are Not Easily Persuaded'

2. **German** – 'Who Is The Authority For This Strength'

3. **Franks** – '(Those Who Are) Definitely Assigned Less'

4. **Goths** – '(The People In) The Marked Off Place'

5. **Roman** – 'Where Is Their Authority To Swing And Spear Not To Live'

6. **Sicily** – 'To Come Upon the Rocks and Boulders'

7. **Norman** – 'It Is So To Take Food From'

8. **British** – 'The Strong Chosen To Do Work Not (With) Wood'

- or -

9. **British** – 'To Pollute An Oath Of Fidelity Without A Woe'

10. **Denmark** – 'That Which Is Soft And Scoured Bright'

11. **Norse** – 'Broken Piece Of Light'

12. **Burma** – 'Wedge'

137

FIGURE III-2-B

DEVELOPMENT OF ENGLISH DEFINITIONS OF NAMES OF
INDIGENOUS PEOPLES AND PLACES FOUND BY
SAMARIANS AND THEIR DESCENDANTS AND BY POST
597 B.C.E. JUDEAN AND JEWISH MERCHANTS DURING
THE FIRST SAMARIAN MILLENNIUM,
8TH CENTURY B.C.E. - 3RD CENTURY C.E.

*When the Samarian Settlers and their descendants traded westward they
apparently came upon a group of people whom they called Teutons. Hard
bargainers for lots of cheap, mostly self indulgent types of goods they were
so named for that characteristic.*

1. Teuton

Jastrow - 524 - p.b.h. - טוֹנְאָ - toonau
                                    - bag, burden, load

Jastrow - 523 - b.h. - טוֹטֶפֶת - totaufet
                                    - something glistening,
                                      beads used for charms,
                                      ornaments worn on the
                                      forehead, frontlet.

טוֹטֶפֶת   טוֹנְאָ

טוֹטֶן - Teuton

NOT!

Jastrow - 109 = אַפְתָּא =פְּתִי - aftau = petee

Jastrow - 1253 - b.h. - פְּתִי - petee
- one easily persuaded,
credulous, inexperienced,
simple

(Those Who Are) Loaded With Charms And Ornaments For Frontlets But Who Are Not Easily Persuaded

----

It appears as though the Samarian Traders and/or their dependents found a group of very well organized people who seemed to have functioned without any particular source of authority and who worked together as a single organized entity; and the Samarians and/or their descendants called them Germans.

2. German

Jastrow - 269 - p.b.h. - גְרַם - gauram
- to be substantial, strong

Jastrow - 723 - p.b.h. - מַאן - man
- who?, what? which? (is the authority for the law)

139

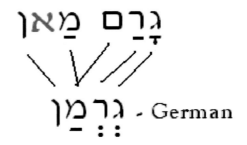

גְּרַם מַאן

גֶּרְמָן - German

NOT!

Jastrow - 1 - א - ah

      -(a prefix) upon, over

A 'NOT!' 'over' would indicate that no one would be in authority.

Who Is The Authority For This Strength

Going further west of the Germans to present day France the Samarians and/or their descendants would have come upon a group of people who appeared to be easily cheated; and the Samarians and/or their descendants called them the Franks.

3. Franks

Jastrow - 1230 - b.h. - פָּרַן - pauran
- to split, break into, to chop, slash, to cut, divide, to assign

Jastrow - 910 - b.h. - נָכָה - naukhau
- to deduct, lessen

פָּרַן נָכָה

פְּרַנְךָ - Frank(s)

NOT!

Jastrow - 327 - b.h. - הַ - ha
-is it not?, behold, indeed

A 'NOT!' 'is it not?' is a definate 'is!'.

(Those Who Are) Definitely Assigned Less

The Goths appeared to have named themselves after the place that they invaded, 'The Marked Off Place'.

4. Goths

Jastrow - 247 - p.b.h. - גַּת - gat
- a marked off place

גַּת

| |

גַּת - Goth (s)

(The People In) The Marked Off Place

When the Samarians and/or their descendants who moved west and then traded south apparently found a group of people who were very free with their weapons, who were out of control in their killing and who seemed to kill randomly. They called those people Romans.

5. Roman

Jastrow - 1461 - b.h. - רוֹמַח - romakh
- to swing, spear

Jastrow - 80 - b.h. - אָן - an
- where? whither (where is
your authority)

רוֹמַח אָן

רוֹמָן - Roman

NOT!

Jastrow - 415 - חָאֵי = חיי - khauee = khae

Jastrow - 454 - b.h. - חיי - khae
- to live

Where Is Their Authority To Swing And Spear Not To Live

Not only did the Samarians and/or their descendants appear to have traded overland and along waterways, but they also traded along sea routes and when they would come upon new places they named them according to their observations of those places. With Sicily being a place covered with rocks and boulders it was named accordingly, 'To Come Upon the Rocks and Boulders'.

6. Sicily

Jastrow - 996 - b.h. - סֶלַע - sela
- rock, clod, boulder

Jastrow - 1081 - b.h. - עָלָה - aulau
- to go up, rise, to
come upon, arrive

143

סֶלַע עָלָה

שְׂ סֶ לָה - Sicily

Jastrow - 1034 - ayeen (עַ) interchanges with heh (הֹ)

To Come Upon the Rocks and Boulders

Sailing out of the Mediterranean Sea and north along the Atlantic coast of Europe the Samarians and/or their descendants would have come upon the coast of France and met the Normans. Normandy then as Normandy now is a good place to grow food, and the traders most certainly would have replenished their supplies from the Normans and so named those people from whom they took food, Normans.

7. Norman

Jastrow - 909 - b.h. - נוֹר - noor
       - to conquer, break ground, clear [to take]

Jastrow - 796 - b.h. - מִן - meen
       - from, of, more (or less) than

Jastrow - 796 - b.h. - מָן - maun
       - portion, food

144

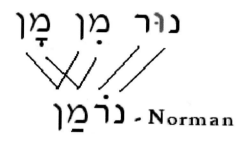

נוֹר מִן כָּן

נֹרמַן - Norman

NOT!
Jastrow - 371 - וֹ - vav
- is it indeed so?

A 'NOT!' 'is it indeed so?' is a strong 'it is indeed so!'.

It Is So To Take Food From

- - - - - - - - - - - - - - - - - - -

On the one hand the Samarians and/or their descendants seemed to have seen the British as strong people doing hard work, but with all of the water around them they didn't build ships with which to engage in trade; meaning that the Samarian Traders would have had to have brought the merchandise to them.

8. British

Jastrow - 198 - p.b.h. - בָּרָתָא - brautau
- the chosen **or** strong

Jastrow - 1124 - b.h. - עָשָׂה - ausau
- to do work, **prepare**

בְּרַתָּא עָשָׂה

בָּרְטִשָׁה - British

NOT!

Jastrow - 99 - b.h. - אָעִי - auee
- wood, woods

The Strong Chosen To Do Work Not (With) Wood

It appears as though after the Samarians and/or their descendants may have brought requested items to some people whom they named British, they perhaps found that those British wouldn't buy those requested items; and so the double entendre name of the people who 'Pollute Their Oath Of Fidelity' appeared to have arisen along with 'The Strong Chosen To Do Work Not With Wood' showing early Britons to have been a very diverse group of people.

9. British

Jastrow - 194 - b.h. - בְּרִית - b'reet
- a ring, band, oath of fidelity

Jastrow - 527 - p.b.h. - טוּש - toosh
- to cover with an adhesive substance, polish, to besmear, soil, pollute

146

בְּרִית טוּשׁ

בְּרְטִשׁ - British

NOT!

Jastrow - 373 - וָֹי - vae
- oh!, woe!

To Pollute An Oath Of Fidelity Without A Woe

Sailing further north along the Atlantic coast of Europe the Samarians and/or their descendants were probably impressed with a particular land for its cleanliness and so they named it such, Denmark, 'That Which Is Soft And Scoured Bright'.

10. Denmark

Jastrow - 315 - p.b.h. - דֵן - daen
- this, that

Jastrow - 846 - b.h. - מָרֵק - mauraek
- to brighten, cleanse
(metal), to scour, scald

Jastrow - 844 - p.b.h. - מָרַךְ - maurak
- to be soft, to soften

147

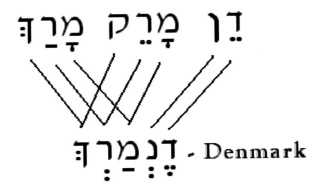

דֶן מָרֶק מָרַךְ

דֶנְמַרךְ - Denmark

That Which Is Soft And Scoured Bright

Sailing further north along the Atlantic coast of Europe the Samarians and/or their descendants would have come to present day Norway which they were probably able to approach only in the summer because of the cold and the ice. The northern reaches of Norway in the summer is 'the land of the midnight sun', where the sun shines at midnight even though it is dark; and that is what they named the country, 'Broken Piece Of Light'.

11. Norse

Jastrow - 936 - b.h. - נוּר - noor
        - light

Jastrow - 1484 - b.h. - רָסֶס - rausaes
        - broken piece

148

נוּר רָסס

נוּרְס - Norse

Broken Piece Of Light

During some period in the history of the Trade Route it expanded tremendously and by the middle of the Second Millennium of the Common Era, corresponding to the end of the Second Millennium of the Samarian Era, there were many trade routes connecting Europe, Asia and South Asia. Two of the largest trading areas for the Samarian Descendants were apparently China and India and in between China and India was Burma, sitting as a wedge between the two giants; and that is what they appeared to have named Burma, 'Wedge'.

12. Burma

Jastrow - 150 - p.b.h. - בּוּרְמָא - boormau
- wedge

בּוּרְמָא
| ן ן ןןן
בּוּרְמָא - Burma

Wedge

149

FIGURE III-3-A

LIST OF DEFINED IN ENGLISH NAMES OF SECOND SAMARIAN MILLENNIUM, 3RD - 13TH CENTURIES C.E., DESCENDANTS, THE BARBARIANS

1. **Barbarian** – '(Here) Is The Uncultivated, Clear, Bright, Clean Son, Not Belonging, (Going)Whither'

2. **Vandals** – 'For If Not The Sons'

3. **Hun** – 'Behold, Here Is Possession And Wealth'

4. **Khazars** – 'To Go Aground Searching'

5. **Anglo** – 'Messenger'

6. **Saxon** – 'Not Over The Proud Enemy'

7. **England** – 'The Angles Where (There) Indeed Is The Leather Bottle (Of Authority)'

8. **Viking** – 'Hunt (For) Dry Soil (With A) Club And Not A Woe'

9. **Valhalla** – 'To Perish (And Go) Further On (To) There'

10. **Eyktorstad** – 'To Go Aground Turn Constantly As A Twisted Band(Under) Broken Control Without Hooks'

11. **Mongols** – 'It Is From A Circle (Of) Exiles'

12. **Merkit** – '(The Tribe That Deals In) Drugs (or Poisons)'

13. **Naiman** – 'The Faithful (or Trustworthy Tribe)'

14. Kereyit – '(The Tribe Coming From) K'reth That Mutilates'

15. Tatar – '(Those Who) Move To And Fro (Who Cut) Not Wood (Like A)Razor'

16. Genghis Khan – 'Thus Overshadowing (All) To Come In Contact (With)!'

17. Temujin – 'The Nature Of The Deity Tammus'

FIGURE - III-3-B

DEVELOPMENT OF ENGLISH DEFINITIONS OF NAMES OF SECOND SAMARIAN MILLENNIUM, 3RD - 13TH CENTURIES C.E., DESCENDANTS, THE BARBARIANS

The name Barbarian, whose definition is typical of the names given themselves by the Second Samarian Millennium Samarian Descendants was apparently coined by a specific group of those descendants to describe themselves; and appears to have been borrowed by the Romans in the 200-500 C.E. time frame and by modern historians to include many militant non-Roman groups whose origins were cloudy.

1. Barbarian

Jastrow - 188 - b.h. - בַּר - bar

- empty, open, uncultivated, living in the wild, prairie, poetic, son, offspring, clear, bright, clean

151

Jastrow - 189 - b.h. - בָּרָאה - baurauau
- external, foreign, not belonging to

Jastrow - 80 - b.h. - אָן - aun
- where?, whither

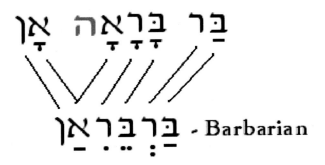

בָּרְבְרַאָן - Barbarian

NOT!

Jastrow - 327 - b.h. - הַ - ha
- is it not?, behold, indeed

A 'NOT!' 'is it not?' is a definate 'is!'.

**(Here) Is The Uncultivated, Clear, Bright, Clean Son,
Not Belonging, (Going)Whither**

152

The Vandals came from where is now modern day Eastern Germany in the Fifth Century C.E. time frame; a region which, during the first centuries of the Common Era the Romans and native Germans fought bloody wars with atrocities on both sides. With the Roman Empire reaching its thousand year point the Vandals came out of their Eastern German territories and went south into the Roman Empire destroying everything that was Roman without apparent cause or reason, bent on merely destroying. Perhaps the tribes that formed the Vandals, the descendants of the earlier victims of Roman cruelty, saw the Roman Empire decaying and their opportunity to get back at the Romans for what the Romans had done to their ancestors centuries before. When we do the Hebrew 'word analysis' on the name Vandal and we come upon the definition, 'For If Not The Sons', we see that the Vandals appear to have been avenging the fate of their ancestors at the hands of the Romans those centuries before and gave themselves an appropriately avenging name.

2. Vandals

Jastrow - 177 - b.h. - בֶּן - baen
          - offspring, son, child

Jastrow - 308 - p.b.h. - דְל - deel
          - for if not

בֶּן דְל

\\ //

בֶּנְדְל - Vandal

For If Not The Sons

- - - - - - - - - - - - - - - - -

Whereas the Vandals apparently came out of their territories for revenge, the Huns came out of their territories in Asia somewhat earlier, in the Fourth and Fifth Centuries C.E. They went west and north across Central Asia, the north shore of the Caspian Sea through modern day Southern Russia just north of or through the northern Caucasus, along the north shore of the Black Sea and into Eastern and Central Europe. Those obviously Samarian descendants wanted a better life and named themselves according to their goal, 'possession and wealth'.

3. Hun

Jastrow - 339 - b.h. - הוֹן - hon
- possession, wealth

Jastrow - 356 - b.h. - הֵן - haen
- here is, behold, they are

הוֹן הֵן

\>✕/

הוּן - Hun

Behold, Here Is Possession And Wealth

154

Along the way from Central Asia to Europe apparently a group, perhaps the Huns, must have camped for a while in the very rich farmland of Southern Russia just north of the Caucasus and in the northern Caucasus between the Caspian Sea and the Black Sea; and the land was so good and so rich and the indigenous peoples perhaps so friendly or obedient that a large number of them stayed as conquering people, as the ruling class; and these were the Khazars. Doing a Hebrew 'word analysis' on the name Khazar we find that these people 'went aground in search of'. They stayed for what appears to have been almost a thousand years, from roughly 300-400 C.E. to roughly 1200 C.E. when, being replaced by the Mongols, they fled to what is present day Ukraine after they had converted to Judaism in 800 C.E.

4. Khazar

Jastrow - 446 - p.b.h. - חֲזַר - khauzar
- to go aground (searching)

חֲזַר
| | |
חֲזַר - Khazar

To Go Aground Searching

Much interaction between peoples during the First Samarian Era, 734 B.C.E. to 266 C.E. brought forth the development of many peoples in Eastern, Northern and Central Europe. One would have expected much infighting with the development of names such as the 'Messengers' and the 'Not Over The Proud Enemies'. In the Fifth and Sixth Centuries C.E., the Barbarian groups of the Angles and the Saxons, the 'Messengers' and the 'Not Over The Proud Enemies', already established in Northern Germany apparently went west to find more and better lands in Britain as the Huns of the Fourth and Fifth Centuries C.E. went west into Eastern and Central Europe; with all groups moving into Roman lands as the Romans were losing control over their empire.

155

5. Anglo

Jastrow - 80 - p.b.h. - אַנְגְלֵי - anglae
- messengers, angels

אַנְגְלִי

אִינְגְלָא - Anglo

Messenger

The Saxons who left Northeastern Germany in the Fifth and Sixth Centuries C.E. for Britain appeared to have developed during the First Samarian Millennium. Also considering themselves the 'new people' they used the more ferocious name of hater, or enemy so as perhaps to intimidate the indigenous and perhaps ferocious peoples of Northern, Central and Eastern Europe rather than the terms of intruders and hostile beings as the 'Stan' peoples of Central Asia called themselves.

6. Saxon

Jastrow - 1550 - b.h. - שַׁחַץ - shakhatz
- proud

Jastrow - 1537 - b.h. - שׂוֹנֵא - sonae
- hater, enemy

שַׁחַץ שׂוֹנֵא

שַׁחְסוֹן - Saxon

Jastrow - 1256 - tsadee (צ, ץ) interchanges with samekh (ס)

NOT!

Jastrow - 1 - א - alef
- upon, over (as a prefix)

Not Over The Proud Enemy

For whatever reason, England was named after the Angles rather than the Saxons with the name England meaning 'this is the authority of the Angles'. The question mark following the root word definition, 'where', gives rise to the question of whether the authority was truly that of the Angles.

7. England

אַנְגְלָא - Anglo

Jastrow - 80 - b.h. - אָן - an
  - where?, whither

Jastrow - 884 - b.h. - נוֹד - nod
  - leather bottle, skin
  [brought to a person
  being administered an
  oath indicating that his
  leather bottle will be
  empty if he violates his
  oath.]

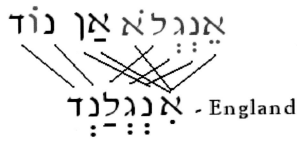

אַנְגְלָנד - England

NOT!
Jastrow - 371 - ו - vav
  - is it indeed so?

A 'NOT!' 'is it indeed so?' is a strong 'it is indeed so!'.

The Angles, Where (There) Indeed Is The Leather Bottle (Of Authority)

~~~~~~~~~~~~~~~~

158

In or around 900 C.E. another group of Barbarian tribes developed in the Northern European and Scandinavian territories occupied by the then Rus peoples. These new Barbarian groups were the Vikings. Unlike most other Barbarian tribes they were described as being heavily involved in trade throughout Eurasia perhaps reflecting their Rus heritage.

8. Viking

Jastrow - 145 - p.b.h. - בּוּכְנָא - bookhaunau
- club

Jastrow - 871 - b.h. - נֶגֶב - negev
- dry soil

Jastrow - 1392 - p.b.h. - קָנִיגִי - k'neegee
- hunter

בּוּכְנָא נֶגֶב קָנִיגִי

בַּנְקָאג - Viking

N OT!
Jastrow - 373 - b.h. - וַיי - vay
- oh! woe!

Hunter (For) Dry Soil (With A) Club And Not A Woe

159

9. Valhalla – The place where Vikings go after they die

Jastrow - 172 - b.h. - בְּלִי - vlee
- to be crumpled, to be worn out, to fail, decay, perish

Jastrow - 352 - b.h. - הָלָא - haulau
- further on

בְּלִי הָלָא
\ ⎮ //
בַּלְהַל - Valhalla

NOT!
Jastrow - 559 - b.h. - יִאַ - yae
- where? whither?

A 'NOT!' 'where?' is a 'there'.

To Perish (And Go) Further On (To) There

‑‑‑‑‑‑‑‑‑‑‑‑‑‑‑‑‑

Eyktorstad, the 'Norse' astronomical term 'whose meaning is difficult to explain', is difficult to explain because it is probably not a Norse astronomical term but it is probably a Viking boat maneuver that puts the boat horizontally onto a beach without the need to use hooks or for the boatmen to enter the water. When interpreting 'twisted band' consider that a steel band when twisted forms a right angle, hence the horizontal maneuver; and a constant turning causes a loss of control.

10. Eyktorstad – Norse astronomical term whose meaning is difficult to explain

Jastrow - 47 - p.b.h. - אֵיךְ - yk
- as, how

Jastrow - 1656 - b.h. - תּוֹר - tor
- turn, order

Jastrow - 1656 - p.b.h. - תּוֹרָא - torau
- row, line, order, twisted band, border

Jastrow - 1566 - b.h. - תּוּר - toor
- to go aground

Jastrow - 1499 - p.b.h. - רְשׁוּת - raushoot
- power, authority, control

Jastrow - 1647 - p.b.h. - תְּדִירָא - t'deerau
- permanently, constantly

Jastrow - 1484 - רְסֵי = רְסַס - r'sae = r'sas

Jastrow - 1484 - b.h. - רְסַס - rausas
- to crush, break into small pieces

161

אִי קְתֹר סְתַד - Eyktorstad

NOT!
Jastrow - 372 - b.h. - וו - vauv
- hook

Jastrow - 372 - b.h. - וו - vauv
- hook

To Go Aground Turn Constantly As A Twisted Band (Under)Broken Control Without Hooks

----

The eastern limit of both the Scythian Empire and what appears to have been the earliest settlements of the abducted Samarians included the western border of modern day Mongolia, the Gobi Desert. By around 1200 C.E. the Mongol tribes, still looking at themselves as 'intruders' as the 'Stan' peoples and 'enemies' as the Saxons did, called themselves the 'Exiles' and came out of Mongolia to conquer most of the Eurasian trade routes and its peoples. Since all of the Mongol names, except for Tatar which could have come in later times, were derived from Biblical Hebrew it is conceivable that their ancestors arrived in 'Mongolia' between 734 and 597 B.C.E. before Aramaic was introduced into the Trade Route. This sets them apart from the other Descendants and so the English definitions of their names are in green.

11. Mongol – The peoples of Mongolia and of the Mongolian Empire

Jastrow - 796 - b.h. - מִן - meen
- from, of, more (or less)
from

Jastrow - 221 - b.h. - גוֹל - gool
- to form a ball, a circle

Jastrow - 221 - b.h. - גוֹלָה - golauh
- exile

מִן גוֹל גוֹלָה

מַנְגוֹל - Mongol

NOT!

Jastrow - 327 - b.h. - ה - is it not?, behold, indeed

A 'NOT!' 'is it not?' is a definate 'it is!'.

It Is From A Circle (Of) Exiles

----

12. Merkit – A Mongol tribe

Jastrow - 847 - b.h. - מְרְקַחַת - meerkkhat
- druggist's preparation,
drug, poison

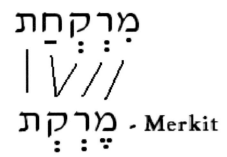

מְרַקַחַת

מֶרְקַת - Merkit

(The Tribe That Deals In) Drugs (or Poisons)

----

13. Naiman – A Mongol tribe

Jastrow - 866 - b.h. - נֶאֱמָן - ne'emaun
- faithful, trustworthy

נֶאֱמָן

נְאַמַן - N'aiman

The Faithful (or Trustworthy Tribe)

----

14. Kereyit – A Mongol tribe

Jastrow - 667 - b.h. - כָּרִית כָּרֵת = כָּרֵת - k'reet

= kauraet

Jastrow - 674 - b.h. - כָּרַת - kaurat
- to cut, mutilate, to cut off, excommunicate

Jastrow - 667 - b.h. - כָּרִית - K'reth
- a district near Philistia

כָּרִית כָּרֵית

כָּרֵית - Kereyit

(The Tribe Coming From) K'reth That Mutilates

----

15. Tatar – A Mongol tribe and the Russian name for Mongol

Jastrow - 1684 - b.h. - תַּעְתַּע - teetae
- to move to and fro, to sport, trifle

Jastrow - 1684 - b.h. - תַּעַר - taar
- razor

165

תְּעַתֵּעַ תַּעַר

תַּתָּר - Tatar

Jastrow - 1034 - ayeen (ע) interchanges with alef (א)
NOT!
Jastrow - 99 - p.b.h. - אעא - auau
- wood, wooden

(Those Who) Move To And Fro (Who Cut) Not Wood (Like A) Razor

----

The conquest by Temujin (the name of Genghis Khan before he became Genghis Khan) over the tribe of Kereyit led by Toghril, Temujin's blood brother and the tribe of Naiman led by another of Temujin's former good friends, Jamuqua, according to Reference 15, is from a story found in 'The Secret History Of The Mongols', an ancient anthology of Ghengis Khan, which parallel's the story in the Bible of David, King Saul and Saul's son Jonathan. In addition, all of the root words found using the Hebrew 'word analysis' on all of the Mongol names are exclusively of Biblical Hebrew origin indicating that the ancestors of the Mongols may have had little to no contact with Aramaic speaking Judean or Jewish merchants or with Samarian Descendants influenced by Aramaic speaking Judean or Jewish merchants, people with Hebrew vernaculars containing Aramaic words acquired after the 597 B.C.E. exile of Judeans to Babylonia. It also appears that these eastern peoples had very little to no cultural contact with other Samarian Descendants after 597 B.C.E. and their mythology should have and appears to have remained very Biblical.

166

16. Genghis Khan – The first Mongol conquering leader

Jastrow - 259 - b.h. - גָּנַה - geenau
- to overshadow, to obscure

Jastrow - 273 - b.h. - גַשׁ = נְגַשׁ - gash = n'gash

Jastrow - 876 - b.h. - נְגַשׁ - n'gash
- to come in contact

Jastrow - 647 - b.h. - כַּן - kan
- so, thus

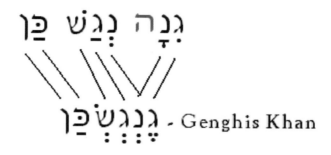

גְּנַגְשׁ כַּן - Genghis Khan

NOT!

Jastrow - 327 - b.h. - הַ - heh
- an interrogatory prefix, 'is it not?'

A 'NOT!' 'is it not?' is a strong is, or an exclamation point (!).

Thus Overshadowing (All) To Come In Contact (With)!

167

17. Temujin – Genghis Khan's original name

Jastrow - 1676 - b.h. - תַּמוּז - tamooz
  - Tammus - name of a deity

Jastrow - 405 - b.h. - זֵן - zaen
  - quality, nature, kind, species

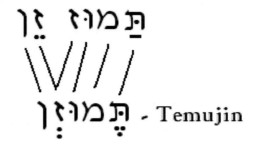

תַּמוּז זֵן

תַּמוּזֵן - Temujin

The Nature Of The Deity Tammus

FIGURE - III-4-A

LIST OF DEFINED IN ENGLISH NAMES AND WORDS OF POSSIBLE NON-DESCENDANTS OF THE SAMARIANS

1. Cossack – '(Those Who) Cut Down'

2. Ataman – 'The Strong (Who) Urges'

3. Stanitsa – 'Urine And Excrement'

FIGURE - III-4-B

DEVELOPMENT OF ENGLISH DEFINITIONS OF NAMES AND WORDS OF POSSIBLE NON-DESCENDANTS OF THE SAMARIANS

The Cossacks appeared to have existed north of the Trade Route with a language similar to those of the Barbarians, derived from ancient Hebrew, with cultural characteristics closely related to those that one would have expected of the Scythians. They didn't appear historically until the Fifteenth Century C.E. after which all of the Barbarians were gone. Since the words ataman and stanitsa contain post Biblical Hebrew root words, the Cossack language development most likely occurred following contact with Samarian Descendants influenced by Aramaic speaking Judean and Jewish merchants.

1. Cossack – The Cossack People

Jastrow - 652 - b.h. - כָּסַח - kausakh
- to cut down

כָּסַח

ן ֹ ן

כָּסָח - Cossack

(Those Who) Cut Down

----

2. Ataman – The leader (Cossack word)

Jastrow - 1063 - p.b.h. - עֳטִי - autee
- urging, instigation

169

Jastrow - 77. - b.h. - אָמֵן - aumaen
- to be strong, enduring

עָטִי אָמֵן

\|\|\/\/\/

אַטָאֵמֵן - Ataman

Jastrow - 559 - yod (י) and ayeen (ע) interchange
with alef (א)

The Strong (Who) Urges

----

3. Stanitsa – Village (Cossack word)

Jastrow - 1639 - b.h. - שָׁתֵן - shautan
- to urinate

Jastrow - 902 - b.h. - נָטֵשׁ - nautash
- to sink, drop, dropping,
excrements

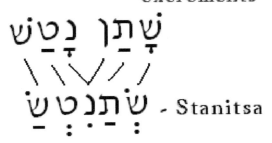

שָׁתֵן נָטֵשׁ

\ \\/\/ /

שָׁתֵנֵטֵשׁ - Stanitsa

Urine And Excrement

170

SECTION IV – CONNECTIONS BETWEEN DESCENDANTS OF THE TEN LOST TRIBES AND EASTERN RELIGIONS

Khorog, according to definition was a place where scholars met and indulged in intoxicating influences. It was and is near the Pamir Mountains and not far from Samarkand, a good source of opium. This was a place most likely where people who used the Trade Route could congregate to philosophize and where the great thinkers of the region, the Samarian descendant scholars, the Eastern scholars and the Middle Eastern and Hebrew scholars could congregate with their peers.

As far as the ancient Eastern scholars are concerned, we have a certain amount of history related to them such as the birth dates and birth places of several founders of eastern religions. For instance, Confucius was born in 551 B.C.E. in Lu, China, now Shantung Province. Buddha Siddhartha, the founder of Buddhism was born between 560 and 448 B.C.E. or between 563 and 483 B.C.E. depending on the source in, it is said, the Kingdom of Sakyas on the border of Nepal and India. Lao Tzu the founder of Taoism was born between 600 and 300 B.C.E.

Taking the average of the age range(s) of each founder puts them all, with some degree of certainty, in their 20's and 30's in the 530 to 520 B.C.E. time frame; about two hundred years after the Samarian abductions and about seventy years after the beginning of the Judean exiles into Babylonia. Enough time for the Samarian Descendant and Hebrew scholars to acquire new words, such as Aramaic words, and be ready to place them into the names and concepts of eastern religions. This was also the time frame during which the Jewish Torah's redaction was begun.

171

FIGURE - IV-1-A

LIST OF EASTERN RELIGIONS' NAMES AND CONCEPTS DEFINED IN ENGLISH

HINDU

1. Hindu – 'Behold Here Is The Devoted Not My Origin'

2. Vedic – '(Those Who) Search, Examine And Investigate'

3. Atman – 'The Solid Part From Thee'

4. Anatman – 'Where Is The Solid Part From Thee?'

5. Samadhi – 'To Cut Off A Portion (Of The Mind)'

6. Karma – 'A Contract (With The) High And Exalted'

7. Brahman – 'Clear, Bright, Clean, And Pure From Thee'

8. Vishnu – 'To Spring Forth Glad Tidings Without Pride'

9. Rama – 'The High Exalted (One)'

10. Krishna – 'The Protector Of People'

11. Havana – 'Proper Conduct (That Is) Half Done'

12. Gopi – 'The Person (Who Had) Illegitimate Intercourse Without A Hook'

13. Shudra – 'Men Of The Field (Working) The Pot That Does Not Overflow'

14. Vishya – '(Those Who Have) Bad Quality (Goods Are) Wicked And Evil!'

BUDDHIST

15. Buddha – 'To Move Nimbly With Clarity'

16. Siddhartha Gautama – 'Joins The Scrapings, Preserves The Ruler Without Favor'

17. Mahamaya – 'Who? Which? What? Anything'

18. Sakyas – 'To Lie Down And Dwell (But) Not (To Be In) The World To Come'

19. Sangha – 'Repetition (Of The) Body (But) It Is Not So'

20. Dharma – 'Eminent Person Who Has Risen Up (Through) The Imposition Of WisdomWithout A Woe'

21. Mahayanas – 'What (Can) Discourage The Providential Event?'

22. Pitaka – 'The Openings (Into The Writings Of Buddha)'

23. Sutta Pitaka – 'The Openings (Into) Moving About And Blowing On The Horns'

24. Vinaya Pitaka – 'The Openings (Into Buddha's Writings On) Building Good Conduct, Refinement And Culture'

25. Yoga – 'To Collect Thoughts (Through) Painstaking Labor As A Sign Of Mental Responsibility Without Always (Being) A Scholar'

26. Mara – 'The Appearance Of Evil Without Its Essence'

27. Bodh Goya – 'Float To The Depression Of Loneliness But Not (Take) The Poison From Her Breast'

28. Nirvana – 'Bather In Light'

TAOIST

29. Tao – 'Not From Reason Or Cause'

30. Wu Wei – 'Hook Pleasure'

31. Zen – 'Learning Without Method'

CONFUCIANIST

32. Yin - CONFUCIANIST & TAOIST – 'To Oppress And Treat Overbearingly, To Vex And Taunt'

33. Yang - CONFUCIANIST & TAOIST – 'To Move Quickly, Glisten, Be Bright, Proud, Haughty And Strong'

34. Karma – 'A Contract (With The) High And Exalted'

FIGURE - IV-1- B

DEVELOPMENT OF ENGLISH DEFINITIONS OF EASTERN RELIGIONS' NAMES AND CONCEPTS

Hindu people were apparently indigenous to the mountain region of Northern India at the time of the Samarians' settlement. The settlers and their descendants were obviously impressed and respectful of those people and as a result named the Hindus for both their faith and their intellect, 'behold here is the devoted'. Although the Samarians and their descendants were impressed with and respectful of the Hindus, they recognized that the Hindus' beliefs were different from theirs.

HINDUISM

1. Hindu

Jastrow - 343 - b.h. - הֵא - hae
- behold, here is

Jastrow - 877 - b.h. - נְדַב - n'dav
- to be devoted to

הֵא נְדַב

\\ /

הֶנְדּוּ - Hindu

NOT!
Jastrow - 2 - p.b.h. - אָב - auv
- my father, my grandfather origin, source

Behold Here Is The Devoted Not My Origin

175

2. Vedic – Another name for Hindu

Jastrow - 141 - b.h. - בָּדַק - baudak
- to search, examine,
  investigate, try

בָּדַק

↓ ↓↓

בְּדֻק - Vedic

(Those Who) Search, Examine and Investigate

In Khorog where the scholars interacted, relationships could have existed in which the Eastern scholars would have described their beliefs and concepts to which the Samarian Descendant and Hebrew scholars would have applied Hebrew and Aramaic Hebrew names to form the following Sanskrit names and names of concepts.

3. Atman – The soul

Jastrow - 43 - p.b.h. - אַטְמָא - atmau
- something solid,
  the solid part

Jastrow - 796 - b.h. - מֵן - meen
- from thee

176

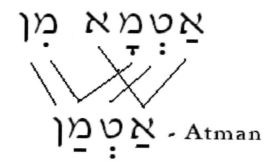

אַטְמָא מִן

אָטְמַן - Atman

The Solid Part From Thee

----

4. Anatman – no self

Jastrow - 80 - b.h. - אָן - aun
- where?, whither

Jastrow - 43 - b.h. - אַטְמָא - atmau
- something solid,
the solid part

Jastrow - 796 - b.h. - מִן - meen
- from thee

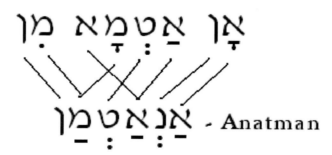

אָן אַטְמָא מִן

אָןאַטְמַן - Anatman

Where Is The Solid Part From Thee?

Comparing the English description of the Hindu concept of Samadhi, 'total collectiveness, no emotion, desire or anger' with the Hebrew 'word analysis' definition, 'To Cut Off A Portion (Of The Mind)', it can be seen that when one 'cuts off' the conscious 'part of the mind' that part which contains no emotion, desire or anger, the subconscious, the part that functions in the purely logical, is allowed to do its job. This process results in a somewhat Mr. Spock (of the Star Ship Enterprise culture) like pure logic mentality.

5. Samadhi – Total collectiveness, no emotion, desire or anger

Jastrow - 1591 - b.h. - שָׁמַד - shaumad
- to destroy, cut off, apostatize, renounce one's religion

Jastrow - 732 - b.h. - מִדָּה - meedau
- dimension, measure, proportion [portion]

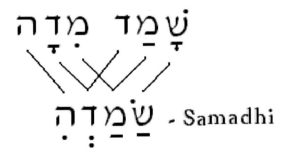

שָׁמַד מִדָּה

שְׁמָדֶה - Samadhi

To Cut Off A Portion (Of The Mind)

178

The Hebrew 'word analysis' definition of the concept of Karma as 'A Contract (With The) High And Exalted' could provide good Karma as meaning the having of a good contract with God and bad Karma as meaning the having of a bad contract with God.

6. Karma – Deed or task

Jastrow - 1421 - b.h. - קָרַם - kauram
- to contract, join, to form a skin cover

Jastrow - 1481 - b.h. - רָם - raum
- high, exalted

קָרָם   רָם   קרם

קְרָם - Karm(a)

A Contract (With The) High And Exalted

The English description of Brahman reads as 'the universal soul, understanding brings enlightenment', and the Hebrew 'word analysis' definition reads as 'Clear, Bright, Clean And Pure From Thee'. Combining both the English description and the Hebrew 'word analysis' definition could result in the statement: 'the universal soul is the understanding and enlightenment which comes from the clarity, brightness, cleanliness and purity that comes from God'.

7. Brahman – The universal soul, understanding brings enlightenment

Jastrow - 189 - b.h. - בַּר - bar
- clear, bright, clean, pure

Jastrow - 796 - b.h. - מִן - meen
- from thee

בַּר מִן
\\ //
בַּרְמַן - Brahman

Clear, Bright, Clean, And Pure From Thee

Vishnu, a Hindu deity, is the preserver who frees the devotees from material desires which can be associated with pride and from the cycle of reincarnation which brings forth glad tidings.

8. Vishnu – A deity, the preserver who blesses devotees with freedom from material desires thus releasing them from the cycle of reincarnation

Jastrow - 198 - b.h. - בְּשׂוֹרָה - b'sorau
- joy, glad tiding, tidings

Jastrow - 883 - b.h. - נוּב - noov
- to spring forth, flow

בְּשׂוֹרָה נוּב

בְּשְׂנוּ - Vishnu

NOT!
Jastrow - 1453 - b.h. - רַהַב - rahav
- pride, greatness, royalty

To Spring Forth Glad Tidings Without Pride

Rama is a reincarnation of Vishnu, the exalted one, and another deity.

9. Rama – An incarnation of Vishnu

Jastrow - 1481 - b.h. - רָם - raum
- high, exalted

רָם
| |
רָם - Ram(a)

The High Exalted (One)

In Krishna we again see a deity in the form of a person, a protector.

10. Krishna – A deity in human form, the charioteer, the protector, the all of everything

Jastrow - 672 - b.h. - כֶּרֶס - keres
- bag, stomach, belly

Jastrow - 1604 - b.h. - שָׂנֵא - saunae
- hate, year, hatred, to repeat, do a second time

כֶּרֶס שָׂנֵא

כֶּרְשָׁנֵא - Krishna

The word hate appeared often to describe a protector as a policeman, so the hater could be the protector and the protector of the stomach or belly could conceivably be a vernacular for the protector of the people.

The Protector Of People

Nowhere in this study of Hindu concepts has there been any sign of real evil. The worst concept found so far has been that of Havana, wicked.

11. Havana – Wicked

Jastrow - 339 - p.b.h. - הַוָנָא - havaunau
    - proper conduct

Jastrow - 865 - b.h. - נָא - nau
    - hurried, half done

הַוָנָא נָא

הַוָנָא - Havana

Proper Conduct (That Is) Half Done

Gopi is the woman who had sex with Krishna most likely without the benefit of marriage. In the naming of Gopi by the Samarian Descendant and Hebrew scholars and the definition from the Hebrew 'word analysis', she was the person who had extramarital intercourse with Krishna where 'without a hook' could mean without marriage.

12. Gopi – The woman who had sex with Krishna

Jastrow - 225 - b.h. - גוּף - goof
    - body, person, self

Jastrow - 225 - p.b.h. - גוף - goof

- to embrace, to have illegitimate intercourse, to commit adultery with

גוף   גוף

גף - Gop(i)

NOT!

Jastrow - 372 - b.h. - וו -vauv

ָ - hook

The Person (Who Had) Illegitimate Intercourse Without A Hook

In ancient as well as in modern times craftspeople were and are often farmers working in the crafts in off season. Their intricate work shows in the definition, 'a pot that does not overflow'. The formers of the word Shudra might have looked at 'a pot that does not overflow' as a fluid under precise thermal control. That precise control is brought into the workplace of craftspeople and is at the root of the process of crafting.

13. Shudra – Craftspeople

Jastrow - 1529 - p.b.h. - שׂוֹדָנִי - soodaunee
- man of the field, sportsman

Jastrow - 283 - b.h. - דוּד - door
- boiler, caldron, pot

שׂוֹדָנִי דוּד

שׂוּדָר - Shudra

NOT!
Jastrow - 902 - b.h. - נִיב - neev
- flow, overflow

Men Of The Field (Working) The Pot That Does Not Overflow

The Samarian Descendant scholars and perhaps Hebrew scholars as well, although they were most likely linked to trade apparently didn't like merchants and so they gave merchants a name meaning bad quality, wickedness and evil. The word beeshoo (בישׁוּ), meaning bad quality, wickedness and evil, is a post Biblical Hebrew word, one that came to the Trade Route with the appearance of the Aramaic speaking Judeans after their exile to Babylonia in 597 B.C.E., indicating that that concept may not have been in the Biblical Hebrew vocabulary.

14. Vishya – Merchants

Jastrow - 167 - p.b.h. - בִּישׁוּ - beeshoo
- bad quality, wickedness, evil

בִּישׁוּ

X ֹ

בְּשִׁי - Vishya

NOT!
Jastrow - 371 - וֹ - vav
- is it indeed so?

A 'NOT!' 'is it indeed so?' is a strong 'it is indeed so!'.

(Those Who Have) Bad Quality (Goods Are) Wicked And Evil!

BUDDHISM

Looking closely at people who are enlightened, it could be seen that those enlightened people express themselves in nimble and clear language.

15. Buddha – The completely enlightened one

Jastrow - 143 - b.h. - בּוֹא - bo

        - to enter into, split, insert, to be vacant, clear

Jastrow - 280 - b.h. - דָּדָה - daudau

        - to move nimbly, hop, trip, to walk, pull

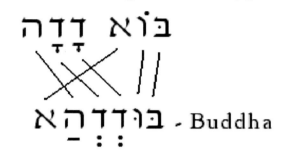

בּוֹדְדַהָא - Buddha

To Move Nimbly With Clarity

Buddha unites the lowly and separated people, the scrapings, and does it without showing favor to any one; and Buddha keeps God.

16. Siddhartha Gautama – One whose aim is accomplished; and is the name of the founder of Buddhism

Jastrow - 956 - b.h. - סדד - sid

        - to join

Jastrow - 501 - b.h. - חָרַט - khaurat

        - to scrape, to chisel

Jastrow - 201 - b.h. - גֵּאֶה - gaeh
- lofty ruler, lord, proud, haughty

Jastrow - 540 - b.h. - טָמַן - tauman
- to hide, store away, preserve

סדד חָרֵט גֵּאֶה טָמַן

סִדְדְהַרְטָא גְטְמָא - Siddhartha Gautama

NOT!

Jastrow - 484 - b.h. - חָנֵן - khaunaen
- to cover, surround, to caress, grace, favor

Joins The Scrapings Without Favor And Preserves The Ruler

The name of Buddha's mother, 'Who? Which? What? Anything', was at first hard to understand but when reading back into the text of the comparative religion book, Reference 7, it was found that Buddha's mother died on the seventh day after his birth. An interesting observation is to look at the compound of the Hebrew words ma (מה) and mee (מי), mahmee, which has a Hebraic sound identical to that of the English slang word mommy.

17. Mahamaya – Buddha's mother, the Queen of Sakya

Jastrow - 736 - b.h. - מָה - ma
- something, anything, what?, which?

Jastrow - 770 - b.h. - מִי - mee,
- who? which?

מַה מִי

| \ / ַ

מַהמִי - Mahamaya

Who? Which? What? Anything

The composition of many of the Hebrew names given to eastern religions' concepts had to have reflected on how the Samarian Descendant and Hebrew scholars apparently thought. 'To Lie Down And Dwell (But) Not To Enter Into The World To Come' is right in line with how the men of that time had to have thought about women, whom the infants were extensions of. They were not important; just there to sleep, eat and relieve themselves and not yet 'in the world to come'. That occurred when they, especially the male children, entered into the world of men.

18. Sakyas – The birthplace of Buddha

Jastrow - 599 - b.h. - יָשֵׁב - yaushaev
- to sit down, rest, to dwell, remain, to be inactive

189

Jastrow - 1570 - b.h. - שָׁכַב - shauchav
- to incline, to lie down, lie, sleep

יָשַׁב שָׁכַב

שָׁכִיש - Sakyas

NOT!

Jastrow - 136 - בַּב = בָּאָה - bauv= beeau

Jastrow - 135 - p.b.h. - בָּקָא = בָּאה' -

Jastrow - 185 - p.b.h. - בָּקָא - bakau
- to enter into, search

Taking liberties by relating the sounds of beeau (בָּאָה) and bau(בָּא) gives:

Jastrow - 134 - b.h. - בָּא - bau
- coming, future, the world to come, futurity

To Lie Down And Dwell (But) Not To Enter Into The World To Come

- - - - - - - - - - - - - - - - - -

A long line of people dressed the same and looking the same could appear as though they were all the same person, but they are not.

190

19. Sangha – An assembly of monks

Jastrow - 1604 - b.h. - שָׁנָה - shaunau
         - repetition, double

Jastrow - 216 - b.h. - גַו - gav
         - belly, body

שָׁנָה גַו

✗//

שַׁנְגְהַ - Sangha

NOT!

Jastrow - 371 - ו - vav

       - a prefix, and, but; often
         introducing a question 'but
         is it indeed so?'

As a positive prefix the vav (ו) would introduce a question, but as a 'NOT!' prefix it would end a statement with an exclamatory negative, ' it is not so!'.

Repetition (Of The) Body (But) It Is Not So

In discussing Dharma, where Dharma in its English description from the Sanskrit is a building block of the world, we could establish the Samarian Descendant and Hebrew scholar definition using the Hebrew 'word analysis' as an 'Eminent Person Who Has Risen Up (Through) The Imposition Of Wisdom Without A Woe'; a person who has increased the knowledge of the world and so has himself risen up in society and in so doing changed the world without considering fate.

20. Dharma – The world is made of building blocks called Dharma

Jastrow - 275 דִי - dee
- prefix of who, which, that

Jastrow - 365 - b.h. - הַר - haer
- mound, mountain, eminent person

Jastrow - 1460 - b.h. - רִים - reem
- to be high, lifted up, to rise

Jastrow - 275 - p.b.h. - דָה - dau
- this, [the word 'this' implies wisdom]

Jastrow - 1482 - b.h. - רְמֵי - r'mae
- to throw, swing, to put on, to impose

דִי הַר רִים דָה רְמֵי

דְּהַרְמַה - Dharma

192

NOT!

Jastrow - 576 - p.b.h. - ‏יי‎ - yee

- oh!, woe!

Eminent Person Who Has Risen Up (Through) The Imposition Of Wisdom Without A Woe

- - - - - - - - - - - - - - - - -

The Hebrew 'word analysis' definition of Mahayanas as 'What (Can) Discourage The Providential Event?', with the providential event most likely meaning fate, raises a possible difference between Dharma, 'a person who has increased the knowledge of the world and so has himself risen up in society and in so doing changed the world without considering fate' and Mahayanas, 'that nothing and no one can interfere with fate' leading to this possible meaning of Mahayanas, 'that nothing and no one can interfere with fate, not even Dharma'.

21. Mahayanas – Say that Dharma is not correct because nothing is permanent or solid

Jastrow - 736 - b.h. - ‏מה‎ - ma

- something, anything, which? what?

Jastrow - 581 - b.h. - ‏ינה‎ - yaunau

- to oppress, treat overbearingly, vex, taunt, to be undecided, discourage

Jastrow - 914 - b.h. - נֵס - naes
- flag, sign, wonder, providential
event

מַה יָנָה נֵס

מֲהִינָס - Mahayanas

What (Can) Discourage The Providential Event?

The 'openings' into Buddha's thoughts should be like the getting into the writings and the understanding of Buddha. A combination of the English description and the Hebrew 'word analysis' definition results in the final Hebrew 'word analysis' definition.

22. Pitaka – The baskets containing the writings of Buddha

Jastrow - 1252 - b.h. - פֶּתַח - petakh
- opening, door, gate

פֶּתַח
| ד /
פֶּתָק - Pitaka

The Openings (Into The Writings Of Buddha)

194

Self deprecation is an attribute in our day and was most probably one in the days of the founding of the eastern religions. Looking at the Hebrew 'word analysis' definition of Sutta Pitaka it appears as though Buddha was a modest man. 'Moving about and blowing on the horns' is what a self deprecating person could say about the communication of his thoughts.

23. Sutta Pitaka – The Basket of Discourse (communication of thoughts)

Jastrow - 962 - b.h. - סוט - soot
- to move about, be unsteady

Jastrow - 523 - p.b.h. - טוט - tot
- blow on the horn

Jastrow - 1252 - b.h. - פֶּתַח - petakh
- opening, door, gate

סוט טוט פֶּתַח

סוט טֻ פֶּק - Sutta Pitaka

Jastrow - 415 - khet (ח) interchanges with koof (ק)

The Openings (Into) Moving About And Blowing On The Horns

What Buddha wrote about people's refinement and culture lay in the Vinaya Pitaka.

24. Vinaya Pitaka – The Basket of Discipline

Jastrow - 176 - b.h. - בָּנָה - baunau
- to build

Jastrow - 176 - p.b.h. - בָּנָאִין - banaueen
- one of becoming conduct, refined, cultured person

Jastrow - 1252 - b.h. - פֶּתַח - petakh
- opening, door, gate

בָּנָה בָּנָאִין פֶּתַח

בְּנִי פְּטַקה - Vinaya Pitaka

Jastrow - 559 - yod (י) interchanges with alef (א)

Jastrow - 415 - khet (ח) interchanges with koof (ק)

The Openings (Into Buddha's Writings On) Building Good Conduct, Refinement And Culture

----

Yoga makes it possible for people through painstaking labor or exercise to utilize their minds without always having to be a habitual learner, a scholar. Note should be taken of the Hebrew word egoz (אגוז) meaning 'nut, as signs of mental responsibility', and its relationship to the English vernacular.

25. Yoga – union

Jastrow - 562 - b.h. - יְגִיעַ - y'geeah
                    - painstaking, labor

Jastrow - 13 - b.h. - אָגַר - augar
                 - to store up thoughts and
                   knowledge, arguments,
                   gather, collect

Jastrow - 11 - b.h. - אֱגוֹז - egoz
                 - nut (as signs of mental
                  responsibility)

יְגִיעַ אָגַר אֱגוֹז

יוֹג - Yoga

NOT!

Jastrow - 1034 - p.b.h. - עָא - au
                 - always

Jastrow - 117 - b.h. - אֶרֶז - erez
                 - prominent men, scholars

To Collect Thoughts (Through) Painstaking Labor As A Sign Of Mental Responsibility Without Always (Being) A Scholar

----

197

The modern English definition for the name Mara, the evil one, doesn't really mean the evil one according to the Hebrew 'word analysis' definition. According to that definition the name Mara is more like 'the one who is wicked'.

26. Mara – The evil one

Jastrow - 835 -p.b.h.- מַרְאִית - mareet
- appearance, sight, semblance (relating to repulsion to look at, and the evil eye)

מַרְאִית

מַר - Mara

NOT!

Jastrow - 61 - b.h.- אִית - eet
- essence, permanent or normal condition

The Appearance Of Evil Without Its Essence

Differences between the direct modern western way of thinking and the more poetic way that the ancients thought can be shown through the comparison of the modern English description from the Sanskrit of the place Bodh Goya, 'where Siddhartha was tempted by Mara the evil one but resisted' and the Hebrew 'word analysis' definition where Siddhartha 'floated to the depression of loneliness but did not take the poison from her breast'.

27. Bodh Goya – Where Siddhartha was tempted by Mara the evil one but resisted.

Jastrow - 139 - b.h. - בָּדָד - baudaud
- loneliness, in a lonely state, in exile

Jastrow - 275 - b.h. - דָאָה - dauau
- to float, fly

Jastrow - 233 - b.h. - גַיְא - gaye
- glen, wady (a depression)

בָּדָד דָאָה גַיְא

גַיְא דָאָה בָּדָד - Bodh Gaya

NOT!

Jastrow - 280 - b.h. - דָדָא - dadau
- she may smear poison on her breast

Float To The Depression Of Loneliness But Not (Take) The Poison From Her Breast

----

The Hebrew 'word analysis' definition of Nirvana comes from a combination of both Biblical and post Biblical Hebrew words indicating that this Hebrew word came after the 597 B.C.E. exile of the Judeans to Babylonia and the interaction of those Aramaic speaking Judeans with the Samarians and Samarian Descendants.

28. Nirvana – Salvation and inner peace, perfect bliss

Jastrow - 936 - b.h. - נֵר - naer
- light

Jastrow - 176 - p.b.h. - בַּנָאָה - banauau
- bather

נֵר בַּנָאָה

\\//

נִרְבְנָה - Nirvana

Jastrow - 327 - heh (ה) interchanges with alef (א)

Bather In Light

TAOISM

The Hebrew 'word analysis' definition of the name Tao, 'Not From Reason Or Cause', appears to relate to fate along with the English description from the Sanskrit also relating to fate, 'the source from which everything comes, to do nothing is to do everything'.

29. Tao – The source from which everything comes, to do nothing is to do everything

Jastrow - 543 - b.h. - טַעַם - ta'am
- pleasure, will, sense, wisdom, sound reasoning, reason, cause, ground

טַעַם

//

טַע - Tao

NOT!

Jastrow - 721 - b.h. - מִי - mee
- from, of

Not From Reason Or Cause

Combining the Hebrew 'word analysis' definition of Wu Wei as gaining pleasure and the English description from Sanskrit as seeming to relate to fate, brings the meaning of 'to do nothing and allow fate to rule is pleasureful'.

201

30. Wu Wei – Action through inaction, or do without doing

Jastrow - 372 - b.h. - וָו - vauv

‎ָ - hook

Jastrow - 372 - b.h. - וָה - vau

‎ָ - an exclamation of pleasure

וָה וּ

‎וָ

‎ו

‎וּ וָה - Voo Vae (Wu Wei)

Hook Pleasure

CONFUCIANISM

'Learning Without Method' and *'to enlighten from ignorance'* appear to be quite synonymous in definition and description.

31. Zen – To enlighten from ignorance

Jastrow - 1290 - p.b.h. - צְנָא - tsanau
- a basket (of palm leaves) [used in various idioms including dates, birds, fruits, books], a man full of learning, but without method

צְנָא

//

זֵן - Zen

Jastrow - 1256 - tsadee (צ) interchanges with zayeen (ז)

Liberties were taken in dropping the aleph (א).

Learning Without Method

- - - - - - - - - - - - - - - - -

The Hebrew 'word analysis' definition of Yin relates to oppression. In the English description from Sanskrit the elements of gender and extreme negativism enter. Combining the two leads to the concept that in those ancient times men considered women to be dark, cold, evil, negative, inactive, resting, reflective, perhaps lazy; and oppressive, overbearing, vexing and taunting.

32. Yin - CONFUCIANISM & TAOISM – dark, female, cold, evil, negative, inactive, rest, reflection

Jastrow - 581 - b.h. - יָנָה - yaunau
- to oppress, treat overbearingly, vex, taunt

יָנָה
וו
יָנָה - Yin

To Oppress And Treat Overbearingly, To Vex And Taunt

Using the combined Hebrew 'word analysis' definition and the English from the Sanskrit description of Yang shows what men in those ancient times might have thought about themselves. They were light, good, warm, positive, bright, proud and haughty. They moved quickly, were active and creative. They glistened; just the opposite of women who were dark, cold, evil, negative, inactive, lazy, oppressive, overbearing, vexing and taunting.

33. Yang - CONFUCIANISM & TAOISM – Light, male, good, warmth, positive, light side, active and creative

Jastrow - 581 - b.h. - יָנַן - yaunan
  - to move quickly, glisten, be bright

Jastrow - 201 - b.h. - גֵאֶה - gaeeh
  - lofty, ruler, lord, proud, haughty

יָנַן גֵאֶה

יָנֵג - Yang

NOT!
Jastrow - 327 - p.b.h. - ה"א - he
  - intimates the weak (left) hand

A 'NOT!' weak hand is a strong hand or a strength

To Move Quickly, Glisten, Be Bright, Proud, Haughty And Strong

----

Confucian Karma is described in English from Sanskrit as destiny. Introducing the Hebrew 'word analysis' definition to the Confucian Karma brings 'A Contract With The High And Exalted'. Combining the English definition and the Hebrew 'word analysis' definition shows that personal action effects destiny as the Confucian meaning of Karma. This seems to differ from the Hindu Karma only slightly with the Hindu Karma seeming to specify an action to effect Karma whereas the Confucian Karma seems to specify an action effecting destiny or perhaps fate with both concepts of Karma requiring an action.

34. Karma – Destiny

Jastrow - 1421 - b.h. - קֶרֶם - kauram
- to contract, join, to form a skin cover

Jastrow - 1481 - b.h. - רָם - raum
- high, exalted

קֶרֶם רָם

קַרְם - Karm(a)

A Contract (With The) High And Exalted

SECTION V – MODERN LANGUAGES RESULTING FROM THE DESCENDANTS OF THE TEN LOST TRIBES

According to Reference 12, page vii many modern languages have been traced through Sanskrit to the ancient and mysterious Indo-European language. Therefore it should be fitting to begin this section on modern languages resulting from the languages of the descendants of the 'Ten Lost Tribes' with Hebrew 'word analyses' of the names of the languages of Sanskrit and Prokrit.

There are English words that are identical in sound to Hebrew words in meanings and in sequence of consonants. Ester (אסתר) and star, shake (שק) and shake, and steppe (שתף) and step are examples. These words have the same sounds, consonantal sequences and meanings both in English and in ancient Hebrew.

Other English words having similar Hebrew 'word analysis' definitions and sounds are advocate, silly and garden.

People's names such as Shakespeare, Turkmen Basii, Tsar and Stalin as well as the names of places associated with the Jewish People such as Israel and Yeb can be defined into logical English meanings using the Hebrew 'word analysis'.

Legendary sightings of 'The Ten Lost Tribes' going to Japan prompted the Hebrew 'word analyses' of familiar Japanese words.

As in Section III, here the names Amerigo Vespucci and Columbus could have come from post 597 B.C.E. Jews using Biblical Hebrew or Aramaic Hebrew even into medieval and more recent times 'as a second language'.

FIGURE - V-1-A

LIST OF NAMES AND WORDS IN AND OF MODERN LANGUAGES RESULTING FROM THE DESCENDANTS OF THE TEN LOST TRIBES DEFINED IN ENGLISH

1. Sanskrit – 'To Separate The Laced'

2. Prokrit – 'To Separate The Bullock'

3. Star – 'Star'

4. Steppes – 'To Join'

5. Shake – 'Shake'

6. Advocate – 'One Who (Does) Others' (Work, Uses) Witnesses, Testimony And Evidence To Shuttle And Weave (A Web), (And) If He Gains, He Gains Little (For Himself), If He Loses, He Loses Much (For Others) Without A Woe'

7. Silly – 'To Draw Wine From The Wine Pit'

8. Garden – 'To Plough Livable Land Here'

9. Tumult – 'To Stir And Be Mixed Up Beyond Time And Recognition'

10. Trollop – 'To Cling (To) Her Sin'

11. Shakeshosse – 'To Knock (Off Fruit With) Prickly Rough Skin Without A Mark'

12. Robin Hood – 'Chief (With) Distinction, Pride and Majesty'

13. Turkmen Basii – 'The Turkmen Who Is Warm, Sweet, Pleasant And Pleasing, Not He'

14. Tsar – 'The Oppressor'

15. Serf – 'The Consumed'

16. Stalin – 'And Why Do We Not Say, Madman?'

17. Israel – 'To Be Firm, Strong, Healthy, Straight And Right On His Own Accord'

18. Yeb – 'To Load (With) A Strong Hand'

19. Amerigo Vespucci – 'Joins The Bodies (Of) Soil, Painted (With) Powdered Colors (To Have) No Calamity, Misery Or Grief'

20. Columbus – 'Caller Without Hesitation (On The) Stand (At The) Entrance'

21. Japan – 'To Turn One's Face And Join Without Apprehension'

22. Samurai – '(The Emperor's) Guards'

23. Tsunami – 'To Be Stung Hard And Soaked In A Bowl'

24. Booshito – 'The Mark (Of) Chastity'

FIGURE - V-1-B

DEVELOPMENT OF ENGLISH DEFINITIONS OF NAMES AND WORDS IN AND OF MODERN LANGUAGES RESULTING FROM THE DESCENDANTS OF THE TEN LOST TRIBES

Sanskrit, an eastern religious language is well structured as differentiated from the commonly spoken language of Prokrit. It has been used from the Third Century B.C.E., is still used in the Northern Buddhist Church and was the basis for the discovery of Indo-European.

The word laced is interpreted here as meaning 'tightly formed', which is what lacing is, and the word bullock is interpreted here as meaning 'crude' and is often used as such in the English vernacular to indicate crudeness.

The tightly formed could relate to sophistication whereas the crude could relate to the unsophisticated. This brings in the separation of the sophisticated from the unsophisticated; the Sanskrit from the Prokrit.

1. Sanskrit

Jastrow - 1607 - b.h. - שׁנס - shnis
- squeeze in, fasten, lace

Jastrow - 674 - b.h. - כָּרַת - k'rat
- to separate

שׁנס כרת
\\\ / / /
שָׁנְסְכְרַת - Sanskrit

To Separate The Laced

210

2. Prokrit

Jastrow - 1212 - b.h. - פַּר - paur
- bullock

Jastrow - 674 - b.h. - כָּרַת - krat
- to separate

פַּר כָּרַת

פְּרְכְּרַת - Prokrit

To Separate The Bullock

A star is a star is a star.

3. Star

Jastrow - 99 - b.h. - אֶסְתֵּר - estaer
- bright star

אֶסְתֵּר

סְתַּר - Star

Liberties were taken in dropping the aleph (א).

Star

211

Using the Hebrew 'word analysis' on the word steppe results in the definition, from the Assyrian, to join. The steppes of Central Asia join Central Asia with Russia, China, India, and the Middle East. Whether steppes join geographically or steps join the levels of a residence or other structure, they all join.

4. Steppe

Jastrow - 1639 - p.b.h. - שֻׁתָּף - shautaf (from the Assyrian)
- to join, combine, attach, to form a partnership

שֻׁתָּף
| | |
שֶׁתֶּף - Steppe

To Join

The word shake was found as a result of doing a Hebrew 'word analysis' on the name Shakespeare. This find was almost miraculous, being made possible by the completeness of the Jastrow Dictionary in cross referencing words that have different sounds but which have the same meanings.

5. Shake

Jastrow - 1626 - קִשְׁקֵשׁ = שִׁקְשֵׁק - sheekshaek
= keeshkaesh

Jastrow - 1431 - p.b.h. - קִשְׁקֵשׁ - keeshkaesh
- to knock, strike, shake

שֵׁק - Shake

Shake

----

*A lawyer is an advocate, and the word advocate as defined using the
Hebrew 'word analysis' has a very rich and complex origin coming probably
from the Angles and the Saxons.*

6. Advocate – From the Old English – pleads a cause

Jastrow - 15 - b.h. - אָדָא - audau
- fowler, one who puts up
bait, snares, for other
people's doves

Jastrow - 145 - b.h. - בּוּכְיָא - bookhyau
- the weaver's shuttle,
the spider

213

Jastrow - 1345 - p.b.h. - קְטָא - ktau
- to pluck, chip, to harvest, fragment (If he gains anything he gains a piece of coal, if he loses he loses a pearl)

Jastrow - 1042 - b.h. - עֵד - aed
- witness, evidence

Jastrow - 1045 - b.h. - עֵדוּת - aedoot
- testimony, evidence

אֲדָא בּוּכְיָא קְטָא עֵד עֵדוּת

אַדְבְּכָת - Advocate

Jastrow - 1034 - ayeen (ע) interchanges with alef (א)

NOT!
Jastrow - 373 - וַוִי - vav
- oh!, woe!

One Who (Does) Others' (Work, Uses) Witnesses, Testimony And Evidence To Shuttle And Weave (A Web), (And) If He Gains, He Gains Little (For Himself), If He Loses, He Loses Much (For Others) Without A Woe

214

It seems as though the modern day usage of the word silly better reflects the Hebrew 'word analysis' definition, 'To Draw Wine From The Wine Pit', than the modern day English definition of 'happy, prosperous, blessed and innocent'.

7. Silly – Happy, prosperous, blessed, innocent. – From the Anglo-Saxon

Jastrow - 1582 - b.h. - שְׁלִי - slee

- to draw out, pull, to draw wine (from the pit)

שְׁלִי
| | |
שְׁלִי - Silly

To Draw Wine From The Wine Pit

----

8. Garden – A garden

Jastrow - 256 - b.h. - גַּן - ga'n

- garden [actually a livable land]

Jastrow - 1452 - b.h. - רְדִי - r'dee

- to subjugate the ground, to plough

גַן רְדִי

גַרְדֵן - Garden

NOT!
Jastrow - 559 - p.b.h. - אַי - yae
-where?

A 'NOT!' 'where?' is a 'here'.

To Plough Livable Land Here

A tumult is a state of confusion.

9. Tumult – Commotion, disturbance

Jastrow - 540 - טָמַע = נִטְמַע - tauma = neetma

Jastrow - 540 - p.b.h. - נִטְמַע - neetma
- to be hidden, sunk, to be mixed up beyond recognition

Jastrow - 720 - p.b.h. - לָתַת - lautat (Arabic)
- to stir, mix

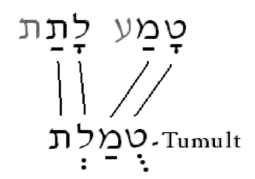

טָמֵע לָתֵת

טָמֵלֵת - Tumult

NOT!
Jastrow - 1128 - b.h. - עֵת - aet
- time

A 'NOT! 'time' is 'without time' or 'beyond time'.

To Stir And Be Mixed Up Beyond Time And Recognition

A trollop in many languages is always a trollop.

10. Trollop – A prostitute

Jastrow - 1656 - b.h. - תּוֹר - tor
- turtle dove [offering brought
to the Temple by a woman
for her sin, a symbol of sin]

Jastrow - 715 - p.b.h. - לָפֵף - lauff
- to cling, to clasp

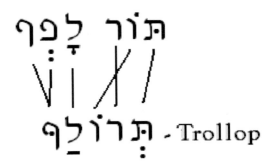

תָּרוֹלַף - Trollop

To Cling (To) Her Sin

There are cacti fruit from the Middle Eastern deserts that are considered delicacies and picking them must be quite an art. The Hebrew 'word analysis' of William Shakespeare's supposed original family name of Shakeshosse shows that the ancestors of the Shakespeare family were most likely desert cactus farmers.

11. Shakeshosse – An alias used by William Shakespeare in or around 1588

Jastrow - 1626 - קָשַׁק שֵׁק = קָשֵׁק שׁק - sheekshaek = keeshkaesh

Jastrow - 1431 - p.b.h. - קָשֵׁק שׁ - keeshkaesh - to knock, strike, shake

218

Jastrow - 1432 - b.h. - קַשְׂקֶשֶׂת - kaskeset
- incision, rough
skin, coat of scales

Jastrow - 340 - b.h. - הוּצָא - hootsau
- prickly

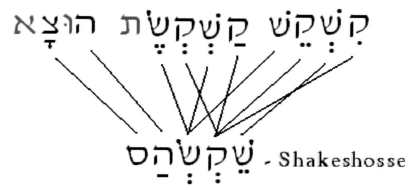

קִשְׂקֵשׂ קַשְׂקֶשֶׂת הוּצָא

שֶׂקֶשֶׂהַס - Shakeshosse

Jastrow - 1256 - tsadee (צ) interchanges with samekh (ס)

NOT!
Jastrow - 1649 - p.b.h. - תָּוָא - t'vau
- mark

To Knock (Off Fruit With) Prickly Rough Skin Without A Mark

- - - - - - - - - - - - - - - - - -

Robin Hood who led a band of para military, socially benevolent followers was possibly an Angle, Saxon, or Anglo-Saxon chief still fighting the Normans during the century after the Norman conquest of 1066 C.E.

12. Robin Hood – The hero of England's Sherwood Forest in the Twelfth Century C.E.

Jastrow - 1444 - p.b.h. - רַבָּן - rabaun
- chief, teacher

Jastrow - 337 - b.h. - הוֹד - hod
- distinction, pride, majesty

הוֹד   רַבָּן
| \ \   ו ו ו
הוד   רַבִּן - Robin Hood

Chief (With) Distinction, Pride and Majesty

Although modern Turkic probably doesn't use the subtraction of loose consonants resulting from the formation of compound words and then introducing those loose consonants into definitions as negative words, it is ironic that using the Hebrew 'word analysis' to define the name of a modern day leader of Turkmenistan, now deceased, Turkmen Basii, the English description from the Turkic, 'The Benevolent Turkmen is transformed, by the leader's own hand, into 'The Turkmen Who Is Warm, Sweet, Pleasant And Pleasing, Not He'.

13. Turkmen Basii – The Benevolent Turkmen – A leader, now deceased, of Turkmenistan

Jastrow - 526 - b.h. - טוֹרַח - torakh
- toil, labor, trouble, painstaking preparations

Jastrow - 796 - b.h. - מָנָה - maunau
- portion, food

Jastrow - 179 - b.h. - בָּשֵׂם - bausame
- be warm, sweet, pleasant, pleasing

טוֹרַח מָנָה בָּשֵׂם

טוּרְקְמֶן בַּשִּׁ - Turkmen Basii

NOT!

Jastrow - 354 - הֶם = הוּא - haem = hoo

Jastrow - 335 - b.h. - הוּא - hoo
- he, it, she, it is

The Turkmen Who Is Warm, Sweet, Pleasant And Pleasing, Not He

----

The first Tsar of Russia was given the name Tsar, which when using the Hebrew 'word analysis' gets the definition of 'The Oppressor'.

14. Tsar – Emperor of Imperial Russia

Jastrow - 1299 - b.h. - צַר - tzar
- oppressor, adversary

צַר

| |

צַר - Tsar

The Oppressor

Whereas the Tsar, the oppressor, imposed the system of serfdom onto certain peasants in Russia, those peasants were consumed by that system.

15. Serf – A class of people in pre – Nineteenth Century C.E. Russia held in a form of slavery

Jastrow - 1632 - b.h. - שָׂרַף - sauraf
- to consume, to burn

שָׂרַף

| | |

שְׂרֶף - Serf

The Consumed

A former dictator of the then Soviet Union named himself Stalin, which described in English takes on the meaning, the 'man of steel'; but when defined in English using the Hebrew 'word analysis' it takes on the meaning, 'And Why Do We Not Say, Madman'?

16. Stalin – Former dictator of the Soviet Union

Jastrow - 1553 - p.b.h. - שָׁטֵי - shautae
- insane, madman, fool, to be demented, to rage

Jastrow - 713 - p.b.h. - לַנְנָן - laun'naun
- and why do we not say?

שָׁטֵי לַנְנָן

שִׁטַלִין - Stalin

And Why Do We Not Say, Madman?

The name Israel connotes the descendants of the Hebrew Patriarch Jacob who took on the name, Israel. The Hebrew 'word analysis' definition of Israel shows Jacob to have been a 'self starter'.

223

17. Israel – The nation of Israel – Another name for the Patriarch Jacob

Jastrow - 601 - b.h. - יָשֵׁר - yausaer
- to be firm, strong, healthy,
to be straight, right

Jastrow - 66 - b.h. - אֶל - el
- to turn to, toward, of itself,
of my or his own accord,
on my or his own authority

יָשֵׁר אֶל
\ \ / / /
יִשְׂרָאֵל - Yisrauael (Israel)

To Be Firm, Strong, Healthy, Straight And Right On His Own Accord

----

It is to be expected that the people who settled in the upper Nile River city of Yeb dealt with heavy loads. They brought gold, ivory, wood and exotic animals from Africa through Yeb to the rest of the then known world. This activity required strong hands to do the loading and carrying.

18. Yeb – The city in Egypt fled to and later named by Judeans escaping the Babylonians in 586 B.C.E.

Jastrow - 560 - b.h. - יַ‎בְ‎ = יְ‎הַ‎ב - yav = y'hav

Jastrow - 565 - b.h. - יְ‎הָ‎ב = יְ‎הָ‎בָ‎א - y'hauv = y'hauvau

Jastrow - 565 - b.h. - יְ‎הָ‎בָ‎א - y'hauvau
- that which is put on, bundle, load on the back, load

יְ‎הָ‎בָ‎א

\ /

יֶ‎בְ - Yeb

NOT!
Jastrow - 327 - b.h. - הַ‎"א - he
- Exodus XIII,16 where 'he' indicates a weak hand

A 'NOT!' 'weak hand' is a strong hand.

To Load (With) A Strong Hand

America was presumably named after the chart maker, Amerigo Vespucci, 1451-1512, who published a map of the then recognized North America. The name of the chart maker, or the company selling the chart, was an advertisement for navigators and sailors to purchase and use the multi-colored chart and so be safe when sailing between continents.

19. Amerigo Vespucci – Fifteenth and Sixteenth Centuries C.E. navigator and map maker

Jastrow - 78 - b.h. - אָמַר - aumar
- to join, knot, an authority

Jastrow - 216 - b.h. - גוֹא - goh
- belly, body

Jastrow - 374 - p.b.h. - וְסִי - v'see (Arabic origin)
- to color, stain, soiled (shoes were soiled with mud)

Jastrow - 1140 b.h. - פִּיחַ = פִּיַיחַ = פּוּחַ
- pooakh = peeyaeeakh = peeakh

Jastrow - 1140 - b.h. - פִּיחַ - peeakh
- to paint, (to use powered colors)

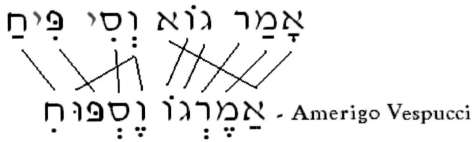

אָמַר גוֹא וְסִי פִּיחַ

אָמְרְגוֹ וְסְפוּחַ - Amerigo Vespucci

NOT!
Jastrow - 576 - p.b.h. - יֵי - yee
- oh!, woe!

A 'NOT!' 'woe!' is 'without woe' or 'without calamity, misery or grief'.

Joins The Bodies (Of) Soil, Painted (With) Powdered Colors (To Have) No Calamity, Misery Or Grief

It appears as though Christopher Columbus' family name was based on the family business of auctioneering. Their workplace as well as that of the bidders was probably on a stand or bridge at a dock exit and/or entrance from which they would call for bids on merchandise being carried on wagons passing below them that had just come off of or was about to be put onto ships.

20. Columbus – The European navigator who found the Western Hemisphere

Jastrow - 1327 - b.h. - קׄול - kol

- voice, call, sound

Jastrow - 724 - b.h. - מָבוׄי - mauvoee

- entrance, gate

Jastrow - 147 - בׄוס = בָּסַׄס - boos = bausas

Taking liberties:

Jastrow - 178 - בָּסַׄס = בְּסַׄס - bausas = b'sas

And:

Jastrow - 178 - בְּסַׄס = בְּסׄיס - b'sas = b'sees

And:

Jastrow - 178 - בְּסׄיס = בָּסׄיס - b'sees = bausees

227

Jastrow - 178 - b.h. - בָּסִיס - bausees
- footstool, stand, base

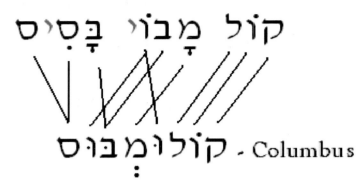

קוֹל מָבוֹי בָּסִיס

קוֹלוּמְבּוּס - Columbus

NOT!

Jastrow - 578 - p.b.h. - יי - yee
- interjection, oh!, woe!

A 'NOT!' 'woe!' could be interpreted as being without hesitation.

Caller Without Hesitation (On The) Stand (At The) Entrance

In many cultures, the keeping of one's 'face' is of paramount importance; and to turn one's 'face' is to 'give in'. The giving in of all of the separate entities making up the 'new' Japanese Islands to a central government, Japan, must have been a large loss of 'face' for the leaders of many of those separate entities.

228

21. Japan – The nation of Japan

Jastrow - 585 - b.h. - יָפֶה - yaupeh
- to join

Jastrow - 1187 - b.h. - פָּנָה - paunau
- to turn (one's face)

יָפֶה   פָּנָה

יָפֶן - Japan

NOT!

Jastrow - 335 - b.h. - הֵה - heh
- ah, alas

A 'NOT!' 'alas' is a lack of apprehension.

To Turn One's Face And Join Without Apprehension

The Samurai were know to have come to Japan in the Tenth Century C.E., three centuries before the great Mongol conquests, and had been serving the Emperor of Japan for the greater amount of time since then. It is conceivable that they could have come from Mongolia since the Samurai resembled the Mongols in many ways.

22. Samurai – To serve – A Japanese class of people who served the Emperor

Jastrow - 1563 - p.b.h. - שִׁימוּר - sheemoor
- guarding, care

שִׁימוּר

שָׁמוּרַי - Samurai

(The Emperor's) Guards

The word tsunami refers to a tidal wave, but its definition using the Hebrew 'word analysis' comes from what happens to the people as a result of the tidal wave.

23. Tsunami – Japanese word for tidal waves that result from underwater earthquakes.

Jastrow - 1292 - b.h. - צָנֻם - tsaunaum
- to sting, be hard, shrunk, shrunk pieces of bread (soaked) in a bowl

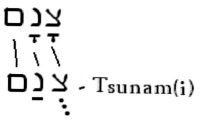

צָנַם - Tsunam(i)

To Be Stung Hard And Soaked In A Bowl

To keep a warrior chaste is to marshall all of his focus and energy into keeping fit, constantly, and being ready for ferocious battle. All of his focus and energy including his sexual energy would therefore be available for combat.

24. Booshito – Japanese 'Code of Warriors'

Jastrow - 151 - b.h. - בּוּשֶׁת - booshet
- shame, insult, bashfulness, chastity

Jastrow - 1663 - b.h. - תָּו - tauv
- mark

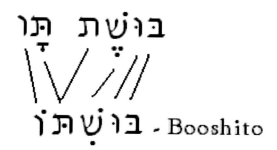

בּוּשֶׁתּוֹ - Booshito

The Mark (Of) Chastity

SECTION VI – ADDITIONAL SUPPOSITIONS

With Sanskrit appearing to have been derived from the ancient Hebrew, as seen here, rather than from the academically accepted somewhat mystical Indo-European language, we must suppose that ancient Hebrew, including Biblical and Aramaic Hebrew should be considered as the language from which German, Swedish, Danish, Norwegian, Icelandic, English, Dutch, Indian, Sanskrit, Armenian, Albanian, Russian, Polish and Lithuanian; the Altaic languages of Mongolian, Tuvan and Buryat; the Tungusic languages; the Turkic languages of Turkish, Kazakh, Uzbek and Kirghiz; the Caucasian languages such as Georgian and Armenian and about forty more and the Uralic languages including Hungarian and Finish were derived.

With Biblical Hebrew as described in this study having been put onto the steppes of Central Asia over 2700 years ago and then Aramaic Hebrew about one hundred and twenty five years later, the flows of peoples and their languages over the millennia should be viewed as having had ancient Hebrew as their source language. From this view it is evident, at least to this author, that Biblical Hebrew is the true 'mother tongue' of the above mentioned languages; and the source Indo-European language having had its beginnings about 6000 years ago should be looked at as not having originated on the steppes of Russia but rather as having been developed in the Mediterranean Sea area with Biblical Hebrew included as one of the daughter languages of that ancient language as well as the Hellenic, Italic and Celtic languages.

In a coffee house in Greenwich Village, New York in the 1960's several young men are sitting around a table discussing eastern religions. There is an Orthodox Jew from Israel, a secular Jew from the United States, a few young men from India and a few young men from China. They are discussing the Hindu, Buddhist, and Taoist religions and Confuciusism and the young Indian and Chinese men are explaining their respective religions in the language of their host country, English, and the young Jewish men are trying to paraphrase the eastern religions' concepts into English.

But! The coffee house isn't in Greenwich Village, New York in the 1960's; it is in Khorog in the 520's B.C.E. and the Orthodox Jew from Israel isn't an Orthodox Jew from Israel but a Judean from Babylonia speaking Aramaic Hebrew. The secular Jew from the United States isn't a secular Jew from the United States but a Samarian Descendant. The nameless young men from India and China are not nameless young men from India and China but are Buddha Siddhartha, Lao Tzu, and Confucius and they are explaining their respective thoughts in the language of their host, Samarian Descendant Hebrew which is also Aramaic Hebrew, or very close to Aramaic Hebrew. They are in fact fashioning new words in Samarian Descendant Hebrew to explain the thoughts and concepts being spresented. What gatherings they must have been.

Legend has it that the abducted Samarian People, the people of the Ten Lost Tribes of Israel, were taken over the Sambatyon River never to be seen again. Using the Hebrew 'word analysis' on the name Sambatyon, the passing beyond the Sambatyon River is interpreted as meaning the passing beyond the living of a Jewish life.

In defining the Sambatyon River, the river over which Jews cannot pass, the word Sabatayon was found in the Jastrow Dictionary, page 949, as a post Biblical Hebrew word with the following definitions.

1. The River Sabbation, said to rest on the seventh day.

2. From Genesis – Let the River 8 prove that the seventh day is the Sabbath.

3. From the Talmud – The Ten Tribes were exiled to within the River 8, whereas Judah and Benjamin were scattered over all lands.

From these definitions the River Sabbation could be interpreted as meaning the flow of the week which ended on the 7th day, the Sabbath. The River 8 then would be the flow past the Sabbath into the 8th day. The Ten Tribes exiled to within the confines of the River 8 would then have been exiled to

233

the confines of a place where there was no Sabbath while the Tribes of Judah and Benjamin, the two tribes remaining after the abduction of the Ten Lost Tribes, and which were scattered over all lands (in the Diaspora) followed the Sabbath.

Another interpretation of the River 8, the river that passes the Sabbath, was found by using the Hebrew 'word analysis' on the word Sabatayon, the river that rested on the seventh day. That process yielded the following definition.

Sabatayon – The river said to rest on the seventh day

Jastrow - 948 - p.b.h. - סָב - sauv
- grey, old, elder, ancestor, scholar

Jastrow - 532 - טִין = טַבָּן - teen = taunan

Jastrow - 541 - p.b.h. - טַבָּן - t'nan
- to moisten, to be jealous, zealous, agitated

סָב בּ טִין
  \\\ / |
סָ בּ טַ יוֹן - Sabatayon

Zealous Scholar

234

Defining the name Sambatyon using the Hebrew 'word analysis' resulted in the following definition.

Sambatyon – The river that Jews cannot pass over

Jastrow - 998 - b.h. - סַם - sam
- drug, medicine, poison

Jastrow - 156 - בְּטֵין = בְּטַן - b'taen = b'tin

Jastrow - 158 - b.h. - בֶּטֶן - beten
- belly

סַם בְּטִין

סַמבְּטִין - Sambatyon

A Poisoned Belly

- - - - - - - - - - - - - - - - -

So, whereas the River Sabbation that rests on the seventh day relates to a 'Zealous Scholar', the River 8, the Sambatyon River that passes the seventh day relates to 'A Poisoned Belly' where a poisoned belly would naturally be a regurgative belly resulting in regurgeration, a rather unscholarly description; and as the zealous scholar relates to the Sabbath, the regurgative belly relates to those who no longer follow the Sabbath.

This leads to the question then as to what the ancient Jewish People were referring when they lamented the Ten Lost Tribes of Israel, the loss of the Tribes to all of humanity or the loss of the Tribes to the Jewish People?

SECTION VII – BIBLIOGRAPHY – /Referenced page numbers in text

1. Baltsan, Hayim: WEBSTER'S NEW WORLD HEBREW DICTIONARY; Macmillan, New York, NY, 1992

/ ii, 27, 65-67

2. Barnavi, Eli: A HISTORICAL ATLAS OF THE JEWISH PEOPLE; Kuperard, London, 1998

/ i, ii, iv, 1-8, 14, 15, 39, 42, 45, 52, 67, 77, 88, 171, 185, 199, 207, 225, 233

3. HAMMOND WORLD ATLAS: Hammond Incorporated, Maplewood, New Jersey, 1978

/ ii, 22-39, 41-45, 48-56, 62-65, 67-92, 94-97, 100, 102-109, 112, 113, 115, 117-122, 124-126, 131, 135, 138, 140, 142-144, 147-149, 153, 155, 156, 159, 171, 175, 212

4. Jastrow, Marcus: A DICTIONARY OF THE TARGUMIM, THE BABLI AND YERUSHALMI, AND THE MIDRASHIC LITERATURE; The Judaica Press, Inc. New York, 1996

/ ii, 10, 22-28, 30-32, 34, 36-39, 41, 43-46, 48-54, 56, 62-71, 73-76, 78-81, 83-87, 89-92, 94, 96, 97, 100, 102, 104-110, 112-115, 117-120, 122, 124, 125, 127, 133-135, 138, 139, 141-149, 151, 153-161, 163-165, 167-170, 175-183, 185-187, 189, 191-207, 210-213, 215-218, 220-227, 229-231, 233-235

5. Kolatch, Alfred J.: THE JEWISH BOOK OF WHY; Jonathan David Publishers, Inc.; Middle Village, New York 11379, 1981, 1995

6. Kolatch, Alfred J.: THE SECOND JEWISH BOOK OF WHY;
Jonathan David Publishers, Inc.; Middle Village,
New York 11379, 1985

7. Polloch, Robert: THE EVERYTHING WORLD'S RELIGIONS
BOOK, Adams Media Corporation, Avon,
Massachusetts, 2002

/171, 175-183, 185-189, 191-206, 210

8. Steinsaltz, Rabbi Adin: THE TALMUD, THE STEINSALTZ
EDITION, A REFERENCE GUIDE;
Random House, New York, 1989

9. Trepp, Leo: THE COMPLETE BOOK OF JEWISH
OBSERVANCE; Behrman House, Inc., Simon &
Schuster, 1980

10. Tryckare, Tre: THE LORE OF SHIPS, page 224; AB Nordbok,
Gothenburg, Sweden, 1975; Crescent Books,
New York

/160, 161

11. Unterman, Alan: DICTIONARY OF JEWISH LORE AND
LEGEND; Thames and Hudson, Ltd., London
1991

/16, 155, 207, 229, 233

12. WEBSTER'S NEW UNIVERSAL TWENTIETH CENTURY
UNABRIDGED DICTIONARY, Second Edition, Simon &
Shuster, Dorset & Baber, 1972

/152, 153, 207, 209, 210, 211, 213, 215-217, 220, 222, 226, 232

13. Wright, Esmond: AN ILLUSTRATED HISTORY OF THE WORLD; Barnes & Noble, 1993

ARCHAEOLOGY MAGAZINE

14. March/April, 2001, LAND OF THE GOLDEN FLEECE (the Republic of Georgia), page 28

/ 47, 48, 73

NATIONAL GEOGRAPHIC MAGAZINE

15. December, 1996, GENGHIS KHAN, page 2

/131, 162-168

16. June 1998, RUSSIA'S IRON ROAD (The Trans-Siberian Railroad), page 2

/94

17. November, 1998, A COMEBACK FOR THE COSSACKS, page 34

/132, 169, 170

18. May, 1999, THE CASPIAN SEA, page 2, Map Supplement

/25-28, 31-38, 43-46, 48, 49, 52-54, 56, 62, 68-70, 73, 75, 76, 78, 79, 81, 83, 85, 86, 90, 91, 112-115, 117-119, 123-127

30. March, 2004, ARMENIA REBORN, page 28

/ 70, 114

REFORM JUDAISM MAGAZINE

31. Spring, 2004, THE JEWS WE DON'T SEE, page 46, JEWS LOST
& FOUND, page 49

/88

32. Fall, 2004, ARDOR FOR ALEPH, PAGE 42

----

33. Personal contact, media articles and documentaries

/ i, 1-2, 49, 69, 70, 76, 94, 115, 120, 131-135, 138, 139, 141-146,
148-149, 151-160, 162, 163, 165, 167, 169, 175, 178, 184, 188,
189, 196, 207, 211, 213, 215-218, 220-224, 226, 227, 229-231

SECTION VIII – INDEX

243

Thank you for having joined me in this 'voyage of discovery'. Please feel free to use the Hebrew 'word analysis' or any other instrument that you may find or develop to go beyond this very early point in the process of discovery of the 'Legacies'.

Don Miller